Dr Sue Shepherd is an Advanced Accredited Practising Dietitian who specialises in providing dietary advice for people with food intolerances. Having been diagnosed with coeliac disease herself, Sue is recognised internationally as a leading expert dietitian in the area of coeliac disease and irritable bowel syndrome. Sue has written four cookbooks, including *Gluten-free Cooking*, which won the Gourmand (Cordon Bleu) Cookbook Award for 'Best Health and Nutrition Cookbook in Australia'.

The Gluten-free Kitchen

SUE SHEPHERD

Photography by Rob Palmer

VIKING
an imprint of
PENGUIN BOOKS

Contents

Introduction 1

Understanding food
  intolerances 2

Plate-free food 5

Salads 27

Four soups 43

Mains 47

Four comforting sides 85

Desserts 89

Four puddings 115

Baking 119

Glossary 154

Acknowledgements 157

Index 158

Introduction

I am so pleased to present my latest collection of recipes, which have been written with one aim in mind: to welcome you into my gluten-free kitchen. I want you to see that having a food intolerance does not condemn you to a life of doing without. These days, we have so many gluten-free products at our fingertips, and I want to show you just how easily these can be transformed into great-tasting food. Every single recipe in *The Gluten-free Kitchen* is completely gluten-free – no modification required.

I haven't kept it a secret that I have coeliac disease, and many people know I am a dietitian, so on many levels this condition has been a big part of my life. And how lucky I am. I'm passionate about promoting all things gluten-free. I know how satisfied my own tastebuds are, and it is important for me that everyone requiring a gluten-free diet is given the opportunity to experience this too.

Many people who have one food intolerance also have sensitivities in other areas. This is why the recipes in *The Gluten-free Kitchen* are suitable for sufferers of the most common types of dietary conditions, including irritable bowel syndrome, fructose malabsorption, lactose intolerance, and intolerances to fructans, raffinose and sorbitol (see pages 2–3). This is good news for families where members suffer from different conditions, which is increasingly common these days. Overall, the recipes are designed to help people with a variety of conditions enjoy their food to the fullest.

I hope you find the recipes on the following pages delicious and easy to prepare, offering something special – not just for those with specific dietary requirements, but for all your friends and family. Most importantly, I hope you will discover just how many foods people with food intolerances can still enjoy.

Best wishes for good health,

Sue Shepherd

Sue Shepherd

Understanding food intolerances

COELIAC DISEASE

- Coeliac disease is a medically diagnosed condition of an intolerance to gluten in the diet. Gluten is the protein component of wheat, rye, barley and oats.

- In people with coeliac disease, gluten causes damage to the linings of the small intestine. As a result, the ability to absorb nutrients is dramatically decreased and people can become very unwell.

- Typical symptoms include bloating, wind, pain, diarrhoea or constipation or a combination of both, fatigue and iron deficiency.

- Coeliac disease is a life-long condition treated by a diet free from all gluten.

- The gluten-free diet permits fruits, vegetables, plain meat, fish and chicken, legumes and lentils, most dairy foods, oils and margarines.

- Breads, pasta and cereals can be made from alternative sources, including corn, rice, soy, potato and tapioca to name a few. There are also many specialty gluten-free products available.

- Whilst every effort has been made to indicate and ensure gluten-free ingredients, it is essential to read the ingredients list of all food products to determine if they are suitable for inclusion in the gluten-free diet. The recipes in this book comply with the Australian gluten-free food standard at the time of printing.

FRUCTOSE MALABSORPTION

- Fructose malabsorption is a condition where the small intestine is impaired in its ability to absorb fructose (a naturally occurring sugar).

- When fructose is not absorbed properly in the small intestine, it can travel through to the large intestine where bacterial fermentation can cause symptoms of irritable bowel syndrome.

- Although fructose is present in one form or another in virtually every fruit, and in many vegetables and grains, not every food source of fructose needs to be avoided by people with fructose malabsorption.

- The most commonly consumed 'problem' foods are:

  Fruits: apple, pear, mango, watermelon, rockmelon, honeydew melon, quince, paw paw and lychee. In excess, the following are problematic: dried fruit, fruit juice and tomato paste.

  Vegetables: onion, spring onion, leek, artichoke, Jerusalem artichoke, witlof, chicory, radicchio and dandelion greens.

  Others: honey, coconut cream, high-fructose corn syrups, inulin and large quantities of wheat. Some people are also sensitive to rye.

IRRITABLE BOWEL SYNDROME

- Irritable bowel syndrome is a condition that affects approximately 15 percent of the population.

- Common symptoms include excess wind (flatulence), abdominal bloating and pain, changes in bowel habits (diarrhoea, constipation or a combination of both). These symptoms fluctuate in their severity from day to day and week to week.

- There is no one diet that will suit every person who suffers from irritable bowel syndrome. The recipes developed for *The Gluten-free Kitchen* avoid ingredients that have been shown to be a problem in people with irritable bowel syndrome, including wheat, excess fructose foods and foods containing fructans, lactose, sorbitol and raffinose.

FODMAP™

FODMAP™ refers to a group of poorly absorbed food molecules that can cause symptoms of irritable bowel syndrome in many people. FODMAP™ foods include wheat, high-fructose foods and also foods containing lactose, sorbitol and raffinose. Recipes that require modification to be low FODMAP™ are indicated throughout the book.

THE RECIPES

- All recipes in *The Gluten-free Kitchen* are suitable for fructose malabsorption, i.e. they do not contain fructans or excess fructose.

- All recipes are wheat free.

- Most recipes are free of lactose, raffinose and sorbitol, or contain only minimal amounts of these.

- Recipes that require modification to be low FODMAP™ are indicated in the recipe.

- Many gluten-free ingredients are now available in the ever-expanding health-food aisles of the supermarket, while some of the more niche products can be found in larger health-food shops. Asian grocery stores are a real treasure chest of gluten-free foods, stocking many items including the flours needed for baking (potato, fine rice, tapioca and so on).

For more information, refer to my previous cookbook, *Gluten-free Cooking* or visit my website: www.coeliac.com.au

Plate-free
food

Balsamic Tomato and Goat's Cheese Bites

These fresh flavours work so well on the crispy flatbread base – they are the perfect nibble to serve with drinks. Gluten-free flatbreads are now readily available in health-food stores or in the bread section of larger supermarkets.

Makes 40–45

5 pieces gluten-free flatbread
3 tablespoons extra virgin olive oil
3 zucchini (courgettes), halved, then sliced with a vegetable peeler
2 tomatoes, finely chopped
2 tablespoons balsamic vinegar
salt and freshly ground black pepper
250 g fetta
200 g goat's cheese
2 tablespoons low-fat milk
2 tablespoons finely chopped oregano

Preheat the oven to 200°C and grease two baking trays. Cut the flatbread into 3 cm × 3 cm squares, place on the baking trays and bake for 5 minutes until crispy. Remove from the oven and transfer to a wire rack to cool completely.

Heat 1 tablespoon olive oil in a small frying pan over medium–low heat, add the zucchini and cook for 2 minutes or until just tender. Place in a bowl with the tomato, vinegar and remaining olive oil, season with salt and pepper and toss until well combined. Cover and refrigerate for 3–4 hours.

Combine the fetta, goat's cheese and milk in a small bowl. Press a teaspoon of the cheese mixture onto the flatbread bases and top with a teaspoon of the tomato mix. Sprinkle with a little oregano and pepper before serving.

Spinach, Cucumber and Mint Dip

This is a light dip with fresh flavours. If you want to make it even lower in fat, omit the olive oil and use low-fat yoghurt – it will still taste delicious. If you are lactose intolerant, this dip should be enjoyed in small quantities.

Makes about 2 cups

1 tablespoon olive oil
300 g frozen chopped spinach,
    thawed and drained
1 small cucumber, finely chopped
1 tablespoon lemon juice
⅓ cup chopped mint
1 cup gluten-free Greek-style yoghurt
salt and freshly ground black pepper

Combine all the ingredients in a bowl and mix together well. Cover and refrigerate for 2–3 hours before serving.

Moroccan Carrot Dip

This dip is lightly spiced and slightly creamy. While it is delicious as a dip, it also makes a tasty filling for gluten-free crepes – I suggest you double the quantity though!

Makes about 1 cup
500 g carrots, cut into 2 cm chunks
2 tablespoons olive oil
3 tablespoons ricotta
1 tablespoon ground cumin
1 tablespoon ground turmeric
salt and freshly ground black pepper

Cook the carrot in a large saucepan of boiling water for about 10 minutes until soft. Drain and set aside to cool slightly.

Add the olive oil and, using a hand-held blender, puree to a smooth consistency. Stir in the ricotta, cumin and turmeric and season to taste with salt and pepper. Cover and refrigerate for 2–3 hours before serving.

Sweet Potato, Cashew and Coriander Dip

I find this dip a little hard to resist. Its full flavour and great texture will have you returning for more.

Makes about 1 cup
500 g sweet potato, peeled and cut into 2 cm chunks
1 cup toasted cashews
2 tablespoons lemon juice
2 tablespoons olive oil
½ cup chopped coriander
salt and freshly ground black pepper

Cook the sweet potato in a large saucepan of boiling water for about 10 minutes until soft. Drain and set aside to cool slightly.

Add the cashews and lemon juice to the sweet potato then, using a hand-held blender, blend until coarsely mashed. Do not over-process. Stir through the olive oil and chopped coriander and season generously with salt and pepper. Cover and refrigerate for 2–3 hours before serving.

Sweet potato, cashew and coriander dip

Vietnamese Rice Paper Rolls

These fresh-flavoured rolls take a little time to prepare, but they are worth it. Deliciously portable, they make a nice addition to a gluten-free lunch box.

Soak the noodles in a bowl of boiling water until soft. Drain and rinse under cold water, then drain again.

Make a dressing by combining the lime juice, fish sauce, brown sugar, chilli and sesame oil in a screw-top jar. Shake well.

Mix together the noodles, chicken, tofu, coriander, mint and dressing. Season and toss to combine. Refrigerate for 2–3 hours to allow the flavours to infuse.

Fill a large flat dish with hot water. Add one rice paper sheet at a time to the bowl and soak for 30–60 seconds until softened. Blot dry on paper towel and spoon 1½ tablespoons of the chicken mixture onto the centre of the sheet. Place a coriander leaf and mint leaf face down on the top edge of the sheet and roll up tightly, folding in the edges. Cover with a moist cloth while you make the rest of the rolls. Cut in half on the diagonal and serve immediately with your favourite dipping sauce.

Makes 12

100 g dried rice vermicelli noodles, broken into 3 cm lengths
2 tablespoons lime juice
1 tablespoon fish sauce
2 tablespoons brown sugar
2 fresh red chillies, seeded and finely chopped
1 tablespoon sesame oil
350 g cooked chicken breast, shredded
100 g firm tofu, chopped
½ cup chopped coriander
½ cup chopped mint
salt and freshly ground black pepper
12 × 22 cm round rice paper sheets
12 coriander leaves, extra
12 mint leaves, extra

Chargrilled Prawns with Spicy Sauce

This dish is easy to prepare and so full of flavour. My advice is to use the freshest, juiciest prawns you can find. The chilli paste is optional, but I think it's a must!

Makes about 25

1 kg uncooked prawns, peeled and
    deveined, tails intact
3 cloves garlic, crushed
3 cm piece ginger, grated
1 tablespoon sesame oil
1 tablespoon finely chopped coriander
½ –1 teaspoon chilli paste (optional)
lime wedges, to serve

Dipping sauce

⅓ cup rice vinegar
1 teaspoon fish sauce
1½ tablespoons brown sugar
1 teaspoon chopped lemongrass
2 kaffir lime leaves, finely shredded

Combine the prawns, garlic, ginger, sesame oil, coriander and chilli paste (if using) in a large bowl. Toss well to combine, then cover and refrigerate for 3–4 hours to allow the flavours to infuse.

To make the dipping sauce, combine all the ingredients in a screw-top jar and shake vigorously. Pour into a small serving bowl.

Heat a barbecue or chargrill to high for a few minutes, then reduce the heat to medium. Grill the prawns for 2 minutes, then turn and cook the other side for 1 minute. Serve with the dipping sauce and lime wedges.

Haloumi, Capsicum and Mushroom Fritters

Salty haloumi is the perfect foil for the vegetables in these tasty fritters. They are delicious on their own, or serve them with salsa or guacamole.

Makes 8–10

100 ml light olive oil
1 red capsicum (pepper), finely diced
200 g button mushrooms, sliced
180 g haloumi cheese, grated
⅓ cup gluten-free plain flour
2 egg whites, lightly beaten
salt and freshly ground black pepper

Heat 2 tablespoons olive oil in a small frying pan over high heat and saute the capsicum and mushroom for 5–6 minutes until tender and slightly charred. Remove from the heat and allow to cool slightly.

Place the cooled capsicum and mushroom mixture, haloumi, flour and egg white in a bowl and stir until well combined. Season with salt and pepper, then set aside to rest for 10 minutes.

Heat the remaining oil in a medium frying pan over medium–high heat. Spoon in 1 tablespoon batter per fritter and cook for 1 minute. Turn over and flatten slightly with the back of the spoon. Cook for a further minute or so until cooked through and golden brown. Transfer the cooked fritters to a plate lined with paper towel to drain any excess oil, and cover with a tea-towel to keep warm while you cook the remaining fritters. Serve warm.

Savoury Mushroom Bites

This is an excellent gluten-free alternative to vol-au-vents, and while I really like the filling in the recipe, you can stuff the mushrooms with just about anything you have to hand.

Preheat the oven to 180°C and grease a baking tray. With a damp cloth, wipe clean the outer skin of the mushrooms and remove the stem. Place on the baking tray.

Combine the olives, sundried tomatoes, basil, olive oil, salt and pepper in a small bowl and puree with hand-held blender (or crush with a mortar and pestle) until smooth.

Spoon ½ teaspoon sauce into each mushroom and bake for 5–10 minutes until warmed through. Remove from the oven, cover with foil and set aside for 2 minutes so the mushrooms sweat and become soft. Remove the foil. Top with a sprinkle of chopped parsley and serve warm.

Makes 15

15 medium button mushrooms
2 tablespoons black olives, pitted
½ cup sundried tomatoes
½ cup basil
1 tablespoon olive oil
salt and freshly ground black pepper
2 tablespoons chopped flat-leaf parsley

Smoked Salmon Rice Balls

Smoked salmon has such a delicious flavour, and it carries beautifully through these rice balls. Only a little smoked salmon is needed, so don't save them for special occasions – enjoy them often!

Makes 20–25

3 cups strong gluten-free vegetable stock
¾ cup arborio rice
100 g smoked salmon, cut into thin slices
1 tablespoon grated lemon zest
125 g cream cheese
1 egg, beaten
1½ cups dried gluten-free breadcrumbs,
    plus extra if needed
canola oil, for pan-frying
lemon wedges, to serve
gluten-free tartare sauce, to serve
    (optional)

Heat the stock in a large saucepan over medium heat, add the rice and cook for about 10 minutes until tender. Drain any excess liquid. While still warm, stir in the smoked salmon, lemon zest and cream cheese and mix well. Transfer to a bowl and cool to room temperature.

Preheat the oven to 150°C. Stir the beaten egg and ½ cup breadcrumbs into the cooled rice mixture – the mixture should now be firm enough to roll into balls about the size of golf balls. Add more breadcrumbs if required.

Pour the remaining breadcrumbs into a shallow bowl, add the rice balls and toss until well coated.

Heat a little canola oil in a frying pan over medium–high heat. Add the rice balls to the pan in batches and cook, tossing regularly, until evenly browned all over. Transfer to a baking tray and keep warm in the oven while you cook the remaining balls. Serve hot with lemon wedges and gluten-free tartare sauce.

Grilled Eggplant Rolls

The fetta and pine nuts provide great texture and flavour in these eggplant rolls.
I am sure you will enjoy every mouthful.

Makes 20

150 g soft fetta
50 g pine nuts, crushed
3 tablespoons chopped basil
1½ tablespoons milk
salt and freshly ground black pepper
3 small eggplants (aubergines)
100 ml olive oil
2 cups baby spinach leaves, rinsed
    and drained

Combine the fetta, pine nuts, basil and milk in a small bowl and stir until well combined. Season with salt and pepper.

Cut the eggplants lengthways into 3 mm thick slices (discard the small edge pieces). Brush the slices with olive oil. Heat a chargrill until hot, add the eggplant slices in batches and cook for 1 minute on each side. Remove from the heat, cover with foil and cool to room temperature.

Spread the fetta mixture over the eggplant slices and top with a few baby spinach leaves. Roll up the eggplant lengthways and secure with a toothpick if necessary. Serve at room temperature.

Pizza Bites

I have not specified a particular brand of gluten-free bread mix as there are so many that will work well here. Or you could use ready-made gluten-free pizza bases and flatbreads, which are now readily available.

Makes 6 small pizzas

3 cups prepared gluten-free bread mix
2 teaspoons olive oil
300 g lean bacon, sliced
2 tablespoons tomato paste
2 cloves garlic, crushed
⅔ cup crushed pineapple, drained
100 g button mushrooms, sliced
½ green capsicum (pepper), thinly sliced
1 cup grated mozzarella

Preheat the oven to 180°C and line two baking trays with baking paper. Trace three 15 cm circles on each tray and set aside.

Make the bread mix according to the packet directions up to the mixing stage. Spoon ½ cup of the mix onto each baking paper circle and spread out with the back of a spoon to form a circle about 5 mm thick. Dip the spoon in water if required. Bake for 15 minutes, or until lightly browned.

Heat the oil in a heavy-based frying pan over medium heat and saute the bacon for 4 minutes or until crispy. Spread 1½ teaspoons tomato paste and a little garlic over each pizza base and top with bacon, pineapple, mushrooms and capsicum. Finish with grated mozzarella and bake for 15 minutes or until the cheese has melted. If you prefer a crispy base, bake directly on the wire rack of the oven. Cut into bite-sized wedges to serve.

Salads

Noodle Salad with Thai Crab Balls

These crab balls are delicious served with the fresh flavours of the noodle salad. If you like, you could also make the balls slightly smaller and serve them as finger food.

Combine the breadcrumbs and fish sauce in a medium bowl. Add the crab meat, coriander, mint, lime juice, garlic and sweet chilli sauce, and season with salt and pepper. Divide the mixture into eight portions, shape into balls and flatten slightly. Set aside on a plate.

Heat the oil in a large non-stick frying pan over high heat and add the crab balls. Reduce the heat to medium–low and cook for 3–4 minutes on each side or until just cooked and golden brown.

Meanwhile, soak the noodles in a large bowl of boiling water until soft. Drain and rinse under cold water, then drain again. Place in a large bowl with the shredded lettuce, snow pea sprouts, mint and sesame oil and toss to combine. Divide among four serving bowls and serve with the crab balls on top.

Serves 4

½ cup dried gluten-free breadcrumbs
2 tablespoons fish sauce
500 g shredded crab meat
2 tablespoons chopped coriander
2 tablespoons chopped mint
⅓ cup lime juice
2 cloves garlic, crushed
1 tablespoon gluten-free sweet chilli sauce
salt and freshly ground black pepper
3 tablespoons sesame oil

Noodle salad

100 g dried rice vermicelli noodles
3 cups shredded iceberg lettuce
1 cup snow pea sprouts
3 tablespoons chopped Vietnamese mint
1 tablespoon sesame oil

Smoked Chicken and Wild Rice Salad

Smoked chicken is one of my favourite foods – it offers such a wonderful depth of flavour to every dish it is used in. In this salad it is complemented perfectly by the golden sweet potato and tangy sundried tomato.

Serves 4–6

2 litres gluten-free chicken stock
100 g wild rice
2 small sweet potatoes, peeled and
    cut into 1 cm cubes
3 tablespoons olive oil
1½ cups shredded smoked chicken
½ cup chopped basil, plus extra leaves
    to garnish
⅓ cup sundried tomatoes, sliced
salt and freshly ground black pepper

Preheat the oven to 180°C.

Bring the chicken stock to the boil in a medium saucepan, add the wild rice and simmer for 20 minutes or until tender. Drain and set aside to cool.

Meanwhile, toss the sweet potato in 1 tablespoon olive oil and place on a baking tray. Bake for about 20 minutes or until tender and golden brown, turning with tongs every 5–10 minutes. Remove from the oven and cool to room temperature.

Combine the cooled wild rice, sweet potato, smoked chicken, basil, sundried tomato and remaining olive oil in a large bowl. Season to taste with salt and pepper. Toss to combine, then cover and refrigerate for 2–3 hours to allow the flavours to merge. Serve at room temperature.

Goodness Salad

I was struggling to come up with a name for this salad, but when you look at the ingredients I am sure you will agree that this nutritious dish is full of goodness.

Serves 4–6

420 g tin corn kernels
1 zucchini (courgette), cut in half and peeled
    with a vegetable peeler
2 tomatoes, finely chopped
410 g tin champignon pieces
100 g mini dill cucumbers, finely sliced
150 g firm tofu, cut into 5 mm cubes
1 cup snow pea sprouts
1 tablespoon gluten-free sweet chilli sauce
1 tablespoon lime juice
1 teaspoon brown sugar
salt and freshly ground black pepper

Combine the corn kernels, zucchini, tomato, champignon, dill cucumber, tofu and snow pea sprouts in a large serving bowl.

Place the sweet chilli sauce, lime juice and brown sugar in a screw-top jar and shake well until the sugar has dissolved. Pour over the salad and toss to combine. Season to taste and serve.

Vietnamese Prawn Salad

I'm a big fan of prawns, and this lovely light salad is one of my all-time favourite ways to enjoy them.

Serves 4

3 cloves garlic, crushed
3 teaspoons finely ground black pepper,
    plus extra to serve
1½ tablespoons lemon juice
1½ tablespoons lime juice
3 teaspoons brown sugar
salt
400 g peeled cooked prawns
6 cups shredded iceberg lettuce
200 g tinned water chestnuts, drained
    and roughly chopped
3 tablespoons chopped mint
½ small fresh red chilli, finely chopped (optional)

In a medium bowl, mix together the garlic, pepper, lemon juice, lime juice, sugar and salt to taste. Add the prawns and stir until well coated in the dressing. Cover and refrigerate for 3 hours.

Combine the shredded lettuce, water chestnuts, mint, chilli (if using), prawns and remaining marinade in a large bowl and toss gently. Arrange the salad on four plates and season with a good grinding of black pepper. Serve immediately.

Vietnamese prawn salad

Thai Chicken Salad

I created this salad to serve at a public function last summer. It was such a hit, I decided then and there to include it in my next cookbook.

Combine the carrot, cabbage, mint, coriander and chicken in a bowl and gently toss together.

Place the dressing ingredients in a screw-top jar and shake vigorously to combine. Pour over the salad and toss until well combined. Serve immediately.

Serves 4

1 large carrot, peeled and coarsely grated
4 cups shredded Chinese cabbage
3 tablespoons chopped mint
3 tablespoons chopped coriander
300 g cooked chicken breast, shredded

Dressing

3 tablespoons lime juice
1 teaspoon grated ginger
2 teaspoons gluten-free soy sauce
1 tablespoon gluten-free sweet chilli sauce
1 tablespoon fish sauce
1 teaspoon finely chopped lemongrass
1 teaspoon brown sugar

Tabbouleh

It is a delight to include this salad in my book. The traditional recipe is far from gluten-free as it contains cracked wheat (burghul). In this version, I've used quinoa, an ingredient you should be able to find in your local health-food store. I hope you take this opportunity to enjoy eating tabbouleh again.

Serves 4–6

⅔ cup dried quinoa
3 large tomatoes, chopped
4 cups finely chopped flat-leaf parsley
3 tablespoons finely chopped mint
1 clove garlic, crushed
3 tablespoons olive oil
3 tablespoons lemon juice
salt and freshly ground black pepper

Bring a medium saucepan of water to the boil and add the quinoa. Stir, bring back to the boil and cook for 10–12 minutes or until just tender. Drain and rinse under cold water, then drain again.

Place the quinoa, tomato, parsley, mint and garlic in a large bowl and mix until well combined. Cover and refrigerate for 2–3 hours.

Combine the olive oil and lemon juice in a screw-top jar and shake vigorously. Pour over the salad and mix with a spoon until well combined. Season with salt and pepper.

Brown Rice Salad with Goat's Fetta

Wholegrain goodness is the theme here. The brown rice and seeds form a great flavour base for this substantial salad, which works well as a meal in its own right. You will need to cook about 2 cups of rice to yield the required amount of cooked rice.

Preheat the oven to 200°C and lightly grease a baking tray.

Combine the lime juice, soy sauce, sesame oil, garlic and brown sugar in a screw-top jar and shake vigorously. Set aside while you prepare the salad, shaking the dressing well every 10 minutes or so.

Place the pumpkin pieces on the baking tray, add the olive oil and toss well to coat. Arrange in a single layer and bake for 30 minutes until tender and lightly golden, turning occasionally. Remove from the oven and cool to room temperature.

Reduce the oven temperature to 180°C and line a large baking tray with baking paper. Place the sunflower and pumpkin seeds on the tray and bake for 4–5 minutes or until starting to turn golden brown. Remove from the oven and cool to room temperature.

Combine the rice, bean sprouts, parsley, mint, pumpkin seeds and sunflower seeds in a large serving bowl. Add the cooked pumpkin pieces and fetta and drizzle with the dressing. Mix together gently until just combined.

Serves 6

⅓ cup lime juice
1 tablespoon gluten-free soy sauce
1 teaspoon sesame oil
1 clove garlic, crushed
½ teaspoon brown sugar
1 kg pumpkin, peeled and cut into 2 cm pieces
2 tablespoons olive oil
3 tablespoons sunflower seeds
½ cup pumpkin seeds
6 cups cooked brown rice, cooled
1 cup bean sprouts
½ cup chopped flat-leaf parsley
1 tablespoon chopped mint
100 g goat's fetta, crumbled

Spinach Salad

I often make this as an alternative to a standard garden salad. The broad range of ingredients come together very simply to create a delicious accompaniment to your meal.

Serves 4

4 cloves garlic, crushed
3 tablespoons olive oil
2 tablespoons balsamic vinegar
2 tablespoons whole-egg mayonnaise
3 hard-boiled eggs, chopped
190 g tinned water chestnuts, drained and chopped
100 g button mushrooms, sliced
3 tablespoons pine nuts
4 cups baby spinach leaves, rinsed and drained
salt and freshly ground black pepper

Place the garlic, olive oil, vinegar and mayonnaise in a screw-top jar and shake vigorously. Set aside while you prepare the salad, shaking the jar for 30 seconds every 5 minutes or so.

Combine the egg, water chestnuts, mushrooms and pine nuts in a bowl.

Place the baby spinach leaves in large serving bowl, add the egg mixture and gently mix together. Drizzle the dressing over the top, season to taste and toss to combine.

Blue Cheese and Walnut Salad

The pear in this recipe complements blue cheese and walnut so well, but is not suitable for people on a low-FODMAP™ diet (see page 3). If you replace the pear with ½ cup sundried tomatoes, the salad will be just as enjoyable.

Serves 4 as a starter

⅓ cup toasted walnuts, chopped
2 tablespoons whole-egg mayonnaise
1 tablespoon red-wine vinegar
1 teaspoon gluten-free Dijon mustard
salt and freshly ground black pepper
3 cups rocket, rinsed and drained
4 cups baby spinach leaves, rinsed and drained
2 corella pears, cored and sliced
150 g blue cheese, crumbled

Place the walnuts, mayonnaise, vinegar and mustard in a screw-top jar. Season with salt and pepper and shake vigorously.

Combine the rocket, spinach leaves, pear slices and blue cheese in a serving bowl. Shake the dressing and pour over the salad just before serving.

Blue cheese and walnut salad

Four soups

When it's cold outside and you want to feel warm and nourished, soups
are the ideal solution. Follow the simple recipes on the following pages,
or mix and match with whatever ingredients you have to hand.

Thick Curried Chicken and Vegetable Soup

Serves 4

2 tablespoons olive oil
700 g pumpkin, peeled and cut into 2 cm pieces
3 carrots, peeled and cut into 1 cm pieces
3 stalks celery, cut into 1 cm slices
2 teaspoons gluten-free curry powder (more if desired)
1.5 litres gluten-free chicken stock
800 g cooked chicken, shredded
⅔ cup white rice
salt and freshly ground black pepper

Heat the olive oil in a large saucepan over medium heat, add the pumpkin, carrot, celery and curry powder and saute for 2–3 minutes until lightly browned.

Increase the heat to medium–high and add the stock, chicken and rice. Bring to the boil, then reduce the heat and simmer, uncovered, for 20–30 minutes, stirring occasionally to break up the pumpkin. Taste, season with salt and pepper and serve.

Lamb and Vegetable Pasta Soup

Serves 4

2 tablespoons olive oil
2 lamb shanks
500 g pumpkin, peeled and cut into 2 cm pieces
300 g swede, peeled and cut into 2 cm pieces
3 carrots, peeled and cut into 1 cm pieces
3 stalks celery, cut into 1 cm slices
1.5 litres gluten-free beef stock
⅔ cup small gluten-free pasta
salt and freshly ground black pepper

Heat the olive oil in a large saucepan over medium heat and saute the lamb shanks until lightly browned on all sides. Remove the shanks from the pan and set aside. Add the pumpkin, swede, carrot and celery to the pan and cook in the remaining oil and meat juices for 2–3 minutes or until lightly browned.

Increase the heat to medium–high, return the lamb shanks to the pan and add the stock. Bring to the boil, then reduce the heat and simmer, uncovered, for about 20 minutes, stirring occasionally to break up the pumpkin and swede pieces. Add the pasta and simmer for a further 10 minutes.

Take out the lamb shanks, remove the meat from the bones and cut into 2 cm pieces. Return to the pan and stir well. Taste, season with salt and pepper and serve.

Potato and Blue Cheese Soup

Serves 4–6

30 g butter
2 cloves garlic, crushed
2 teaspoons chopped thyme
1 large celeriac, peeled and chopped into small pieces
500 g pontiac potatoes, peeled and chopped into small pieces
2 litres gluten-free vegetable stock
125 g strong blue cheese
salt and freshly ground black pepper

Melt the butter in a large saucepan over medium heat, add the garlic, thyme, celeriac and potato and cook, stirring, for 5 minutes or until the vegetables are lightly browned. Add the stock and bring to the boil. Reduce the heat and simmer for 30 minutes until the celeriac and potato are tender. Take the pan off the heat and leave for 5 minutes.

Using a hand-held blender or food processor, puree the soup to a smooth consistency. Return to the pan (if using a processor) and add the cheese, stirring until melted and mixed through. Reheat over low heat for 3–5 minutes, then season and serve. Recipe pictured on pages 42 and 43.

Laksa

Serves 4

150 g dried rice vermicelli noodles
200 g thick flat rice noodles
2 tablespoons sesame oil
3 teaspoons chopped lemongrass
1 teaspoon shrimp paste
2 teaspoons chilli paste
1 tablespoon gluten-free curry powder
2 cups gluten-free chicken stock
600 g chicken thigh fillets, cut into thin strips
100 g deep-fried tofu puffs, cut in half on the diagonal
2 cups light coconut milk*
½ cup roughly chopped coriander

Break the noodles into 10 cm lengths. Place the noodles in a bowl and cover with boiling water. Soak for 5–10 minutes or until tender, then drain and set aside.

Heat the sesame oil in a large saucepan over medium heat and cook the lemongrass, shrimp paste, chilli paste and curry powder for 1–2 minutes, stirring to develop the flavours. Increase the heat, add the chicken stock and bring to the boil, then reduce the heat and simmer for 5 minutes. Add the chicken and tofu puffs and simmer for a further 5 minutes. Reduce the heat to low and stir in the coconut milk and softened noodles. Ladle the soup into four bowls, top with a sprinkle of chopped coriander and serve immediately.

* People with fructose malabsorption should replace the coconut milk with the same quantity of evaporated milk plus ½ teaspoon coconut essence.

Mains

Beef in Red Wine Marinade

The red wine marinade gives the beef a wonderfully robust flavour. Serve this simple yet flavoursome dish with steamed greens and mashed potato.

Place the steaks on a large baking tray. Combine the wine, olive oil, stock powder, garlic and ½ cup water in a bowl and season with salt and pepper. Pour the marinade evenly over the steaks. Turn the steaks over and gently shake the baking tray to ensure each steak is well covered with marinade. Cover and refrigerate for 2 hours or overnight.

Heat a barbecue grill or chargrill pan to high. Drain the steaks and grill for 1–2 minutes each side, or until cooked to your liking.

Serves 6

6 × 150 g porterhouse or scotch
    fillet steaks
½ cup red wine
2 tablespoons olive oil
1 tablespoon gluten-free beef
    stock powder
2 cloves garlic, crushed
salt and freshly ground black pepper

Rice-Crusted Cheese and Bacon Quiche

I'm always looking for gluten-free alternatives to traditional pastry. Here, I've used rice as the basis for the crust as it adds extra flavour as well as texture.

Serves 6–8

3 cups cooked long-grain rice, warm
1 egg
2 tablespoons finely grated parmesan

Filling
200 g lean bacon, diced
4 eggs, lightly beaten
⅓ cup light cream
2 tablespoons gluten-free Dijon mustard
150 g grated cheddar
salt and freshly ground black pepper

Preheat the oven to 170°C and grease a 23 cm flan tin.

Combine the cooked rice, egg and parmesan in a bowl. Press into the base of the flan tin to a thickness of about 5 mm and bake for 15 minutes or until just starting to turn golden brown.

Meanwhile, to make the filling, saute the bacon in a small frying pan over medium–low heat until just crispy. Remove and drain on paper towel.

Mix together the egg, cream, mustard and cheddar in a bowl until well combined. Add the bacon and season with salt and pepper. Pour into the rice crust and bake for 15–20 minutes or until set and cooked through.

Asian Duck Risotto

Although risotto is a traditional Italian dish, it works really well in this Asian-inspired variation. Chicken may be used instead of duck, if preferred.

Place the five-spice powder, coriander, cumin, garlic, ginger and 2 tablespoons sesame oil in a bowl and mix to form a thin paste. Toss the duck pieces through the paste until well coated, then cover and refrigerate for 3 hours.

Heat the stock in a medium saucepan over low heat and keep it covered at a low simmer.

Heat the remaining sesame oil in a large saucepan over medium heat and cook the duck for 3–4 minutes or until golden and cooked through. Remove with a slotted spoon and set aside.

Add the olive oil and arborio rice to the pan and stir until the rice is well coated in the oil. Add 1 cup hot stock, stirring until it has been completely absorbed. Repeat this process, adding ½ cup of stock at a time, until all but last ½ cup of stock has been used and the rice is tender. This will take about 20 minutes.

Add the duck pieces, vegetables, soy sauce and remaining stock and cook for a further minute or until the vegetables and duck are warmed through. Taste, then season with salt and pepper before serving.

Serves 4–6

1½ teaspoons Chinese five-spice powder
1½ tablespoons chopped coriander,
    plus extra leaves to garnish
½ teaspoon ground cumin
1 clove garlic, crushed
1 tablespoon grated ginger
3 tablespoons sesame oil
500 g duck fillet, sliced
1.5 litres gluten-free chicken stock
2 tablespoons olive oil
2 cups arborio rice
1 carrot, cut into thin strips
½ green capsicum (pepper), thinly sliced
    into 2 cm lengths
½ red capsicum (pepper), thinly sliced
    into 2 cm lengths
½ cup bamboo shoots
1 cup bean sprouts
3 tablespoons gluten-free soy sauce
salt and freshly ground black pepper

Satay Chicken Skewers

Everybody loves satay chicken, and you can adapt this recipe to suit the occasion. Serve with steamed rice as a main meal or place smaller pieces of chicken on toothpicks and enjoy as bite-sized nibbles.

Makes 12

2 teaspoons gluten-free cornflour
¾ cup water
⅓ cup crunchy peanut butter
2 cloves garlic, crushed
1 tablespoon gluten-free soy sauce
1 tablespoon brown sugar
700 g chicken fillet, cut into strips
lime wedges, to serve

In a small saucepan, blend the cornflour with a little water to form a paste. Add the remaining water and mix until smooth. Stir in the peanut butter, garlic, soy sauce and sugar and cook over medium heat until thickened, stirring constantly. Set aside.

Soak 12 wooden skewers in water for 10 minutes to prevent scorching.

Thread the chicken strips onto the skewers and brush thickly with the satay sauce. Cook under the grill, in a chargrill pan or on the barbecue for 2 minutes each side or until cooked through. Serve with lime wedges.

Shepherd's Pie

I researched the origins of this dish and discovered that my family didn't have anything to do with it! I still love it though, and this is my gluten-free FODMAP™-friendly slant (see page 3) on an old 'family' classic.

Serves 4
non-stick cooking spray
3 teaspoons olive oil
400 g lean minced beef
⅔ cup frozen peas and corn mix
1 carrot, grated
⅓ cup gluten-free gravy powder
4 large potatoes, peeled and quartered
40 g butter
⅓ cup low-fat milk, plus extra if needed
salt and freshly ground black pepper

Preheat the oven to 180°C and spray a 1 litre baking dish with non-stick spray.

Heat the olive oil in a medium saucepan over medium heat. Add the beef, vegetables, gravy powder and 1 cup water and cook over medium heat until the meat has browned and a thick gravy has formed.

Cook the potatoes in a saucepan of boiling water for about 10 minutes until soft. Drain and return to the pan. Add the butter and milk and mash to a smooth consistency. Season with salt and pepper, and add more milk if required.

Spoon the meat mixture into the baking dish and top with the mashed potato. Bake for 20–25 minutes or until the mash is golden.

Shepherd's pie

Beef Stroganoff

A sure-fire hit for the whole family. This classic dish with its creamy tomato sauce is delicious served with rice or gluten-free pasta and your choice of vegetables.

Serves 4
600 g lean beef, sliced
2 tablespoons gluten-free cornflour
2 tablespoons vegetable oil
400 g button mushrooms, sliced
1 teaspoon gluten-free beef stock powder
3 tablespoons tomato paste
1 cup light sour cream

Toss the beef strips in cornflour until lightly coated. Heat the oil in a frying pan over medium heat and saute the beef and mushrooms for 3–4 minutes until the beef is starting to brown and the mushrooms have softened.

Mix together the stock powder, tomato paste and sour cream in a small bowl, add to the pan and stir until well combined. Reduce the heat and cook, covered, for 10–15 minutes until the sauce has reduced and thickened slightly.

Ginger Pork Noodles

Rice vermicelli noodles can sometimes contain wheat flour so check the packet carefully to ensure you don't get caught out unexpectedly.

Serves 6

300 g dried rice vermicelli noodles
1 tablespoon sesame oil
2 cloves garlic, crushed
1 teaspoon finely chopped ginger
400 g pork steak, thinly sliced
1 carrot, cut into thin strips
1 bunch bok choy, leaves separated
    and washed
1 cup bamboo shoots
½ cup baby corn
½ cup sliced water chestnuts
2 tablespoons gluten-free soy sauce
1½ tablespoons gluten-free cornflour
600 ml gluten-free chicken stock

Soak the noodles in a large bowl of boiling water until soft. Drain and rinse under cold water, then drain again and set aside.

Heat the sesame oil in wok or frying pan and saute the garlic, ginger and pork. Add the vegetables and stir-fry for a couple of minutes until the vegetables are tender.

Combine the soy sauce and cornflour in a bowl to form a paste. Add the chicken stock and mix until well combined. Pour into the pan and heat gently until the sauce has thickened. Add the noodles and stir until just combined, then serve immediately.

Chicken, Mushroom and Tarragon Pasta

Chicken and tarragon are a fantastic flavour combination. Be sure to use fresh tarragon, otherwise you will miss the full potential of this great-tasting dish.

Serves 6–8
500 g gluten-free pasta
2 tablespoons olive oil
3 cloves garlic, crushed
400 g button mushrooms, sliced
400 g chicken thigh fillets, cut into
    small pieces
3 tablespoons dry white wine
½ cup light cream
½ cup chopped flat-leaf parsley
½ cup chopped tarragon
salt and freshly ground black pepper
3 tablespoons shaved parmesan

Cook the pasta in a large saucepan of boiling water until just tender. Drain and return to the pan. Toss through a little olive oil and cover to keep warm.

Heat the remaining olive oil and garlic in a large heavy-based saucepan over medium heat. Add the mushrooms and chicken and cook for 3–4 minutes until golden. Add the wine and cook for 3 minutes or until the wine has reduced slightly. Stir in the cream, parsley and tarragon, then taste and season with salt and pepper.

Divide the pasta among serving bowls, spoon the sauce over the top and finish with a sprinkle of shaved parmesan.

Spanish Meatballs

Minced lamb is the base ingredient for these meatballs, but you could also use beef or chicken. The flavoursome combination of Spanish spices complements most types of meat.

Serves 8

750 g minced lamb

⅓ cup dried gluten-free breadcrumbs

2 eggs, beaten

2 cloves garlic, crushed

3 tablespoons chopped flat-leaf parsley

salt and freshly ground black pepper

1–2 tablespoons olive oil

fresh herbs and grated parmesan,
    to garnish (optional)

Tomato sauce

1 tablespoon olive oil

2 cloves garlic, crushed

1 teaspoon sweet paprika

¼ teaspoon cayenne pepper

2 × 440 g tins crushed tomatoes

150 g chargrilled capsicum (pepper),
    finely chopped

2 tablespoons red wine

2 teaspoons sugar

salt and freshly ground black pepper

Combine the lamb, breadcrumbs, egg, garlic, parsley, salt and pepper in a large bowl. Using wet hands, shape the mixture into 24 golf-ball-sized meatballs. Cover and refrigerate for 1 hour.

Heat 1 tablespoon olive oil in a large non-stick frying pan over medium heat. Add half the meatballs and cook for 6–8 minutes, turning to ensure they are evenly browned and cooked through. Remove from the pan and keep warm while you cook the remaining meatballs, adding another tablespoon of oil if necessary. Remove the meatballs from the pan and set aside.

To make the sauce, heat the oil in a medium frying pan over medium–low heat and saute the garlic, paprika and cayenne pepper for 1–2 minutes to develop the flavours. Add the tomato, capsicum, red wine and sugar. Stir well, then reduce the heat and simmer for 10 minutes. Add the meatballs and continue to cook for a further 10 minutes until the sauce has thickened. Season well with salt and pepper and serve with creamy polenta (see recipe page 86). Garnish with fresh herbs and grated parmesan, if desired.

Salmon in White Wine Sauce

One of my dear friends, Caitlyn, cooks salmon so well I always request it when she has me over for dinner. When I decide to cook salmon, I serve it with this white wine sauce, which seems to complement the flavour of the fish beautifully.

Serves 4
25 g butter
4 × 230 g salmon fillets, skin on
1 cup dry white wine
60 g chilled butter, extra, cut into 2 cm cubes
1 tablespoon chopped dill
salt and freshly ground black pepper

Heat the butter in frying pan over medium–high heat until melted and foaming. Add the salmon fillets, skin-side down, and cook for 2–3 minutes. Turn and cook the other side for a further 2–3 minutes or until cooked to your liking. Keep warm while you make the sauce.

Bring the wine to the boil in a medium frying pan over high heat. Reduce the heat to medium–low and simmer until reduced by half. Whisk in the extra butter, one cube at a time, ensuring it is melted and well combined between additions. Add the dill and season with salt and pepper.

Place the salmon fillets on warmed plates and pour the white wine sauce over the top. Serve with mashed potato and steamed vegetables or salad.

Salmon in white wine sauce

Spicy Chicken Drumsticks

This simple spice blend adds real character to the chicken drumsticks. You could also use drumettes and make this a messy, hands-on dinner for the family.

Serves 6
3 cloves garlic, crushed
1 tablespoon brown sugar
2 teaspoons ground turmeric
½ teaspoon gluten-free curry powder
1 teaspoon ground coriander
⅓ cup sesame oil
2 kg skinless chicken drumsticks
non-stick cooking spray

Combine the garlic, sugar, spices and oil in a bowl or jug and pour into a large plastic bag. Add the chicken drumsticks and toss to coat well. Tie the bag in a knot, place on a plate and refrigerate for at least 3 hours, or overnight.

Preheat the oven to 180°C and lightly spray a baking tray with non-stick spray.

Transfer the chicken pieces to the baking tray and bake for 15–20 minutes or until cooked through. Serve with steamed rice.

Snapper, Macadamia and Lemon Risotto

The inspiration for this risotto came from a meal I enjoyed recently in Broome, overlooking Cable Beach. It offers a great range of flavours and textures in every mouthful.

Serves 6

1 tablespoon olive oil
⅓ cup lemon juice
1 tablespoon finely grated lemon zest
2 cloves garlic, crushed
2½ cups arborio rice
2 litres gluten-free vegetable stock
½ cup white wine
400 g snapper, cut into small strips
½ cup macadamias, crushed and toasted
½ cup grated parmesan
3 tablespoons chopped flat-leaf parsley
salt and freshly ground black pepper

Heat the olive oil, lemon juice, lemon zest and garlic in a large saucepan. Add the rice and stir for 1–2 minutes until the rice is well coated.

Heat the stock in a saucepan over low heat and keep covered at a low simmer. Add the wine to the rice and cook until absorbed. Add 1 cup of the hot stock, stirring until it has been completely absorbed. Repeat this process, adding ½ cup of stock at a time, until all but the last ½ cup of stock has been used. Add the snapper, macadamias, parmesan and parsley, then the remaining stock and cook until the stock has been absorbed and the snapper is cooked through. Taste, then season with salt and pepper. Serve immediately.

Beef and Mushroom Meatloaf

Meatloaf is a family favourite. Serve it with a fresh salad for a light lunch, or with creamy mashed potato for a hearty dinner.

Serves 4
non-stick cooking spray
750 g lean minced beef
300 g button mushrooms, finely sliced
½ cup gluten-free gravy, made up to the
    consistency of tomato paste
¾ cup dried gluten-free breadcrumbs
2 eggs, lightly beaten
3 cloves garlic, crushed
½ cup chopped flat-leaf parsley
salt and freshly ground black pepper

Preheat the oven to 180°C. Line a 20 cm × 10 cm loaf tin with foil and spray with non-stick spray.

Combine all the ingredients in a large bowl and mix well with your hands. Press into the loaf tin and bake for 40–45 minutes or until cooked through. Leave in the tin for 5 minutes before turning out and cutting into thick slices.

Beef and mushroom meatloaf

Sesame Seafood Stir-fry

If you love seafood, this is the dish for you. The Asian flavours in the marinade complement the vegetables and seafood to create a most enjoyable light meal.

Serves 6
500 g firm white fish fillets, sliced
200 g scallops
300 g uncooked prawns, peeled and deveined, tails intact
1 clove garlic, crushed
1 teaspoon grated ginger
3 tablespoons gluten-free soy sauce
3 tablespoons sushi vinegar
2 tablespoons sesame oil
250 g dried rice vermicelli noodles
250 g snow peas (mange-tout), topped and tailed
200 g broccoli, cut into small florets
1 teaspoon gluten-free Dijon mustard
1 tablespoon brown sugar
2 tablespoons sesame oil, extra
2 tablespoons sesame seeds, toasted

Place the fish pieces, scallops, prawns, garlic, ginger, soy sauce, vinegar and sesame oil in a large bowl and toss to combine. Cover and refrigerate for 2 hours.

Soak the noodles in a large bowl of boiling water until soft. Drain and rinse under cold water, then drain again and set aside.

Heat a large frying pan over high heat. Add the seafood mixture, reserving the marinade, and saute for 2 minutes until just cooked. Add the snow peas and broccoli and cook until tender.

Combine the reserved marinade with the mustard, sugar and extra sesame oil and pour over the seafood and vegetables, stirring well. Add the noodles and sesame seeds, toss gently until warmed through, then serve immediately.

Chicken Parmigiana

Dried gluten-free breadcrumbs are now readily available, but if you'd rather make your own, process a few slices of stale gluten-free bread to fine breadcrumbs in the food processor.

Serves 4

½ cup gluten-free cornflour
2 eggs, lightly beaten
1 cup dried gluten-free breadcrumbs
salt and freshly ground black pepper
4 × 150 g skinless chicken breast fillets
canola oil, for pan-frying
420 g tin crushed tomatoes, drained
2 tablespoons chopped flat-leaf parsley
1 teaspoon sweet paprika
2 teaspoons sugar
½ cup sliced black olives
1 cup grated light cheddar

Preheat the oven to 180°C.

Set out three shallow bowls. Place the cornflour in one bowl, beaten egg in another, and combine the breadcrumbs with some salt and pepper in the third bowl. Coat the chicken pieces in the cornflour, dip in the egg, then toss in the breadcrumbs until well coated.

Heat the canola oil in a large frying pan over medium–low heat. Cook the chicken fillets for 3–4 minutes each side or until golden brown.

Meanwhile, place the crushed tomato, parsley, paprika, sugar and olives in a small frying pan and cook slowly over medium–low heat for 10 minutes, stirring occasionally.

Place the chicken fillets in a baking tray, cover with the tomato sauce and sprinkle with grated cheese. Cover and bake for 15 minutes until the cheese is melted and golden. Serve with a green salad.

Pasta Bolognaise

I have adapted this classic recipe so that it is onion free. Now everybody on a low-FODMAP™ diet (see page 3) can enjoy this family favourite.

Serves 4

500 g gluten-free pasta
1 tablespoon olive oil
800 g lean minced beef
200 g rindless bacon, diced
2 cloves garlic, crushed
2 teaspoons cayenne pepper
½ teaspoon chilli powder
3 tablespoons red wine (optional)
700 ml pureed tomato
200 g mushrooms, sliced
3 tablespoons sliced black olives
salt and freshly ground black pepper
grated parmesan, to serve

Cook the pasta in a large saucepan of boiling water until just tender. Drain and return to the pan. Toss through 2 teaspoons olive oil and cover to keep warm.

Heat the remaining oil in a large heavy-based frying pan over medium heat. Add the beef, bacon and garlic and saute until the beef has browned. Add the cayenne pepper, chilli powder, red wine (if using), pureed tomato, mushrooms and olives and simmer over medium heat for 10 minutes, stirring occasionally. Taste, then season with salt and pepper. Divide the pasta among serving bowls, spoon the sauce over the top and finish with a sprinkling of parmesan.

Barbecued Coriander and Pepper Lamb

Coriander and pepper is a great combination and adds a delicious flavour to the meat. It's well worth asking your butcher to butterfly the lamb for you.

Serves 6
2 tablespoons coarsely ground
    black pepper
2 tablespoons ground coriander
⅓ cup olive oil
1.3 kg lamb shoulder, butterflied
salt

Combine the pepper, ground coriander and olive oil in a small bowl or mortar and pestle. Using a pastry brush, heavily coat the lamb with the seasoned oil and season with salt. Transfer to a plate, cover and refrigerate for at least 3 hours or overnight.

Preheat the oven to 200°C.

Preheat a barbecue, chargrill pan or non-stick frying pan over high heat and cook the lamb on all sides until browned. Place in a roasting tin and finish off in the oven for 20 minutes or until cooked to your liking. Cover with foil and rest for 15 minutes before cutting into thick slices to serve.

Five-spice Chicken Stir-fry

Chinese five-spice powder is one of my favourite spice blends. It complements the chicken beautifully in this simple stir-fry.

Heat 1 tablespoon sesame oil in a wok over medium heat. Add half the chicken pieces and cook until just browned. Remove and keep warm while you cook the remaining chicken pieces.

Blend the cornflour and soy sauce to form a paste. Add 1 cup water and stir to combine. Add the brown sugar, star anise and five-spice powder and stir well.

Heat the remaining oil in the wok and cook the garlic until golden brown. Add the chicken and sauce. Bring to the boil, then reduce the heat to low and cook, covered, for 15 minutes, stirring occasionally. Increase the heat to high, add the capsicum and cook until just tender. Toss through the bean sprouts and serve immediately with steamed rice.

Serves 8

3 tablespoons sesame oil
1 kg chicken thigh fillets, diced
1½ tablespoons gluten-free cornflour
3 tablespoons gluten-free soy sauce
¾ cup brown sugar
3 whole star anise
1½ teaspoons Chinese five-spice powder
2 cloves garlic, crushed
½ green capsicum (pepper), sliced
½ red capsicum (pepper), sliced
1 cup bean sprouts

Curried Kangaroo

Kangaroo is not commonly eaten, but I urge you to try it. The meat is very lean and tender, and is rich in iron, zinc and protein. If you can't find it, the recipe works just as well with beef.

Serves 4

1 tablespoon canola oil
1 teaspoon grated ginger
1 tablespoon gluten-free curry powder
2 cloves garlic, crushed
1 teaspoon sweet paprika
1 teaspoon ground turmeric
2 teaspoons garam masala
2½ cups gluten-free beef stock
400 g potatoes, peeled and cut into
    1 cm cubes
250 g eggplant (aubergine), cut into
    1 cm cubes
700 g kangaroo fillet, thinly sliced
2 tablespoons gluten-free cornflour
3 cups baby spinach leaves, rinsed
    and drained

Heat the oil in a large saucepan over medium heat. Add the ginger, curry powder, garlic, paprika, turmeric and garam masala and saute for 1–2 minutes until fragrant. Increase the heat, add the beef stock and bring to boil, then reduce the heat. Add the potato and eggplant and simmer for 5-6 minutes, or until the potato is just tender.

Toss the kangaroo in the cornflour until lightly coated. Add the kangaroo strips to the pan and stir until just cooked. Add the spinach and cook gently until warmed through. Serve with rice.

Sweet and Sour Chicken

Generally, sweet and sour dishes are not recommended for people with coeliac disease as the chicken is often battered. It may also be unsuitable for a low-FODMAP™ diet (see page 3) because of the onion and fruit content. If you feel that you've been missing out, try this variation.

Preheat the oven to 150°C.

Combine the egg whites and 1½ tablespoons cornflour in a bowl and mix with a wooden spoon, making sure there are no lumps.

Heat the oil in a wok over medium–high heat until slightly smoky. Dip a few slices of chicken at a time into the batter, allowing any excess to drain away. Gently lower the chicken into the hot oil and deep-fry for 1–1½ minutes until pale golden. Remove with a slotted spoon and drain on a plate lined with paper towel. Keep warm in the oven while you cook the remaining chicken pieces.

Reduce the heat to medium and remove all but 1 tablespoon oil from the wok. Stir-fry the capsicum, zucchini and pineapple until the vegetables are just tender.

In a small saucepan, combine the remaining cornflour with a little pineapple juice to form a paste. Stir in the lemon juice, chicken stock and remaining pineapple juice. Bring to the boil, then reduce the heat and simmer for 3–5 minutes, stirring constantly until the sauce thickens.

Add the thickened sauce to the wok and stir until the vegetables are well coated. Stir in the warm chicken and serve with steamed rice.

Serves 4

3 egg whites
2½ tablespoons gluten-free cornflour
1 cup canola oil
400 g chicken thigh fillets, cut into slices
1 red capsicum (pepper), cut into
    1.5 cm pieces
1 green capsicum (pepper), cut into
    1.5 cm pieces
2 zucchini (courgettes), halved lengthways
    and cut into 5 mm slices
225 g tin pineapple pieces, drained,
    reserving 3 tablespoons of the juice
3 tablespoons lemon juice
1 cup gluten-free chicken stock

Spinach and Ricotta Lasagne

Rice paper sheets may be used in place of the gluten-free lasagne, if preferred. For each layer of pasta, you will need to stack three sheets of rice paper (soak them first in hot water until softened).

Serves 8
500 g cooked chopped spinach
500 g low-fat ricotta
1 egg, lightly beaten
2 cloves garlic, crushed
salt and freshly ground black pepper
1 litre low-fat milk
3 tablespoons gluten-free cornflour
3 cups grated low-fat cheddar
500 g packet gluten-free lasagne sheets
1 cup pureed tomato

Preheat the oven to 180°C.

Combine the spinach, ricotta, egg and garlic in a bowl and season with salt and pepper.

In a bowl, combine 3 tablespoons milk with the cornflour to form a paste. Add the remaining milk, mixing well until smooth. Pour into a saucepan and cook over medium heat, stirring constantly, until thickened. Do not boil. Add the grated cheddar and stir until melted.

Prepare the lasagne sheets according to the packet directions and place a layer of sheets on the base of a lasagne dish. Spread half the spinach and ricotta mixture evenly over the sheets. Top with a third of the cheese sauce and ½ cup pureed tomato. Add another layer of lasagne sheets, then the remaining spinach and ricotta mixture, followed by half the remaining cheese sauce and the remaining pureed tomato. Add a final layer of lasagne sheets and the rest of the cheese sauce. Bake for 30 minutes or until golden brown.

Olive and Fetta Veal Steaks

False modesty aside, these steaks taste sensational. Serve them simply with salad and freshly baked gluten-free bread and let the flavours speak for themselves.

Serves 4
150 g black olives, pitted and chopped
200 g fetta, crumbled
1 tablespoon finely grated lemon zest
2 tablespoons chopped mint
2 tablespoons chopped flat-leaf parsley
3 tablespoons olive oil
4 × 150 g lean veal steaks
salt and freshly ground black pepper

Combine the olives, fetta, lemon zest, mint, parsley and 2 tablespoons olive oil in a large bowl. Add the veal steaks one at a time and toss until well coated. Season well with salt and pepper. Set aside on a plate, then cover and refrigerate for at least 3 hours or overnight.

Heat the remaining olive oil in a frying pan over medium heat and pan-fry the veal steaks for 3–5 minutes each side or until cooked to your liking. Serve with salad greens tossed with lemon-infused olive oil.

Olive and fetta veal steaks

polenta

Four comforting sides

A hearty casserole or a perfectly cooked piece of meat
or fish needs a partner on the plate, and the recipes on
the following pages are a few of my favourite stand-bys.

Garlic and Herb Polenta Bake

Serves 8

3 cups gluten-free vegetable stock
1 cup instant polenta
2 cloves garlic, crushed
1 cup chopped fresh herbs (such as parsley,
    sage, thyme and oregano)
3 tablespoons grated parmesan
30 g butter
3 tablespoons grated parmesan, extra

Preheat the oven to 180°C and line a 15 cm × 15 cm baking dish with baking paper.

Bring the stock to the boil in a medium saucepan. Pour in the polenta and cook over medium heat for 3–5 minutes, stirring constantly. The mixture should be very thick. Stir in the garlic, chopped herbs, parmesan and butter, then pour into the baking dish. Smooth the surface and sprinkle with the extra parmesan.

Bake for 10–15 minutes or until the cheese is melted and golden brown. Cut into triangles to serve.

Creamy Polenta

Serves 4

3 cups low-fat milk (use lactose-free milk
    if lactose intolerant)
2 cloves garlic, crushed
2/3 cup instant polenta
salt and freshly ground black pepper

Heat the milk and garlic in a medium saucepan until almost boiling. Add the polenta and stir until the mixture boils, then reduce the heat to low and cook, stirring constantly, for 8–10 minutes until cooked. The polenta should have the texture of smooth mashed potato. Season to taste and serve. Recipe also pictured on page 84.

Tomato, Basil and Bocconcini Pasta Bake

Serves 6

500 g gluten-free pasta spirals
2 tablespoons olive oil
⅔ cup grated parmesan
250 g baby bocconcini balls, cut in half
½ –1 cup roughly chopped basil
500 ml pureed tomato
salt and freshly ground black pepper
3 tablespoons grated parmesan, extra

Preheat the oven to 200°C and lightly grease a 25 cm × 25 cm baking dish.

Cook the pasta in a large saucepan of boiling water until just tender. Rinse under cold water and drain.

Combine the cooked pasta, olive oil, parmesan, bocconcini, basil and most of the pureed tomato (reserve 3 tablespoons) in a large bowl, and season to taste with salt and pepper. Press into the baking dish, smooth the surface and spread with the reserved pureed tomato. Sprinkle with the extra parmesan and bake for 15 minutes or until the cheese is melted and golden. Remove from the oven and rest for 10 minutes before serving.

Fried Rice

Serves 4–6

2 cups long-grain rice
3 tablespoons sesame oil
3 cloves garlic, crushed
1 tablespoon grated ginger
1 carrot, cut into thin strips
¾ cup frozen peas
½ cup tinned corn kernels
½ cup bamboo shoots
1 cup bean sprouts
4 eggs, lightly beaten
3 tablespoons gluten-free soy sauce
salt and freshly ground black pepper

Cook the rice until just tender. Drain, and set aside.

Heat 1 tablespoon sesame oil in a large frying pan over medium heat and briefly saute the garlic and ginger. Add the carrot, peas, corn, bamboo shoots and bean sprouts.

Make a well in the centre of the frying pan, add the beaten egg and stir until just cooked, breaking up the egg as it cooks. Continue to cook until the vegetables are tender. Stir in the rice, then add the soy sauce and remaining sesame oil. Taste, season with salt and pepper and serve.

Desserts

Cinnamon Semifreddo with Berries

Cinnamon lends itself beautifully to sweet dishes. This frozen delight tastes great with berries, but shards of chocolate or toffee also work well. If you are lactose intolerant, this dessert should be enjoyed in small quantities.

Serves 8–10
2 eggs
4 egg yolks
¾ cup caster sugar
600 ml thickened cream
1 teaspoon ground cinnamon
1 cup fresh berries (blueberries, raspberries or chopped strawberries)

Line a 9 cm × 19 cm loaf tin with plastic film, allowing extra to hang over the sides.

Place the eggs, egg yolks and caster sugar in a heatproof bowl and beat with electric beaters for 2–3 minutes, or until fluffy and at least doubled in volume. Set the bowl over a saucepan of simmering water, ensuring the bowl does not touch the water, and beat for a further 6–8 minutes until the mixture is thick, pale and creamy. Remove the bowl from the heat and beat for an additional 2 minutes, or until the mixture has cooled.

Clean the beaters and whisk together the cream and cinnamon until soft peaks from. Gently fold in the egg mixture. Pour into the prepared tin, cover with plastic film and place in the freezer for at least 6 hours (preferably overnight) to set.

When ready to serve, remove the semifreddo from the freezer and set aside for 2–3 minutes before inverting onto a serving plate. Top with fresh berries.

Stewed Rhubarb in Ginger Syrup

Rhubarb is such a versatile vegetable – yes, I said vegetable! I love it in a crumble, in a pie, or served with this ginger syrup. I'm sure you will enjoy it too.

Serves 4
500 g rhubarb, stalks trimmed and cut into 3 cm pieces
½ cup sugar
5 cm piece ginger, thinly sliced
3 tablespoons crushed pistachios

Bring a saucepan of water to the boil, add the rhubarb and simmer for about 5 minutes until tender. Drain, then rinse under cold water and drain again. Set aside.

Combine the sugar, ginger and 2 cups water in a small saucepan and simmer, stirring, over low heat for 2–3 minutes or until the sugar has dissolved. Increase the heat to high and boil without stirring for 5 minutes until the syrup has thickened slightly. Remove from the heat and stir in the rhubarb.

Transfer to a bowl, then cover and refrigerate for at least 3 hours to let the flavours infuse. Serve warm or cold with a sprinkle of pistachios and some ice cream on the side.

Stewed rhubarb in ginger syrup

Lemon Custard Tart

A zesty lemon tart is always a popular dessert. This one uses a set custard filling, which I just love.

Serves 10

130 g fine rice flour
75 g gluten-free cornflour
45 g debittered soy flour
1 teaspoon xanthan gum (optional)
3 tablespoons caster sugar
160 g cold butter
120 ml iced water
pure icing sugar, for dusting
whipped cream, to serve

Lemon filling

2 cups milk (use lactose-free milk
    if lactose intolerant)
3 eggs
⅓ cup lemon juice
3 tablespoons finely grated lemon zest
½ cup caster sugar

Sift the flours and xanthan gum (if using) three times into a bowl (or mix well with a whisk to ensure they are well combined). Process the flours, sugar and butter in a food processor until the mixture resembles fine breadcrumbs. Continue processing, adding 1 tablespoon iced water at a time, until a soft dough forms. Turn out onto a gluten-free floured board and knead for about 3 minutes until smooth. Wrap in plastic film and refrigerate for 30 minutes.

Grease a 23 cm fluted tart dish. Roll out the pastry between two sheets of baking paper to a thickness of 3 mm. Ease into the tart dish and trim the edges, then refrigerate for a further 30 minutes.

Preheat the oven to 170°C.

Line the pastry case with baking paper and fill with baking beads or rice. Blind-bake for 10–15 minutes or until golden brown, remove from the oven and set aside to cool.

To make the filling, pour the milk into a medium saucepan and bring to a simmer over medium–low heat. Remove from the heat. Place the eggs, lemon juice, lemon zest and sugar in a jug and whisk with electric beaters on low speed until just combined. Increase the beater speed and whisk the hot milk into the egg mixture.

Pour the filling into the cooled pastry case and bake for 15–20 minutes or until firm to touch. Remove from the oven and set aside to cool. Dust with icing sugar if desired, and serve with whipped cream.

Low-fat Passionfruit Cheesecake

I have replaced traditional cream cheese with cottage cheese in this recipe, making it significantly lower in fat than regular cheesecake. The passionfruit adds a wonderful tart freshness, but you could also use lemon, lime or berries. Unfortunately, this is not suitable for those who are lactose intolerant.

Line the base and sides of a 22 cm springform cake tin with baking paper.

Place the biscuits in a food processor and process to form fine crumbs. Add the melted dairy spread and process until well combined. Press the biscuit mixture into the base of the tin and refrigerate for 20–30 minutes.

Preheat the oven to 160°C. Bake the biscuit base for 10–15 minutes until lightly golden. Remove from the oven and cool.

Combine the gelatine powder and boiling water in a small heatproof bowl. Set the bowl over a larger bowl of boiling water, stirring constantly until the gelatine has dissolved.

Clean the bowl of the food processor. Add the cottage cheese and condensed milk and blend until smooth. With the motor running, pour in the dissolved gelatine liquid, blending until the mixture is smooth and well combined. Stir in the passionfruit pulp with a metal spoon. Pour the filling over the biscuit base and chill in the refrigerator for at least 3 hours until set. Spoon the extra passionfruit pulp over the cheesecake just before serving.

Serves 10

200 g plain sweet gluten-free biscuits
60 g low-fat dairy spread, melted
1 tablespoon gelatine powder
100 ml boiling water
500 g low-fat cottage cheese
400 g tin skim sweetened condensed milk
pulp from 4 passionfruit or 150 g tinned passionfruit pulp
3–4 passionfruit or 100 g tinned passionfruit pulp, extra, to serve

Baked Chai Latte Cheesecake

Chai latte is normally enjoyed as a beverage, but here it is the feature flavour in this sensational baked cheesecake. This is not suitable for those who are lactose intolerant.

Serves 10
200 g plain sweet gluten-free biscuits
80 g butter, melted
500 g cream cheese
300 ml cream
¾ cup caster sugar
40 g gluten-free chai latte powder
3 eggs, at room temperature
thickened cream, to serve

Line the base and sides of a 20 cm springform cake tin with baking paper.

Place the biscuits in a food processor and process to form fine crumbs. Add the melted butter and process until well combined. Press the biscuit mixture into the base of the tin and refrigerate for 20–30 minutes.

Preheat the oven to 160°C.

Clean the bowl of the food processor and add the cream cheese, cream, sugar and chai latte powder. Blend until smooth. With the motor running, add the eggs, one at a time, processing well between additions.

Pour the filling over the biscuit base. Bake for 45 minutes, then cover with foil and bake for a further 10 minutes or until just firm in the centre. Turn off the oven and leave the cheesecake to cool in the oven with the door ajar for 2 hours (the top of the cheesecake may crack but this won't affect the taste). Remove from the oven and cool in the refrigerator for 4 hours.

Spread cream over the chilled cheesecake just before serving.

Berries in Liqueur Syrup

The Cointreau makes this a decadent adults-only dessert, however it could be omitted to make it suitable for the whole family to enjoy.

Serves 8
¾ cup caster sugar
3 tablespoons Cointreau
4 cups fresh berries (choose from raspberries, boysenberries, blueberries or chopped strawberries)

Combine the sugar and ½ cup water in a medium saucepan over high heat. Bring to the boil, then reduce the heat to medium–low and simmer, stirring constantly, for 5–8 minutes until the sugar has dissolved. Remove from the heat and set aside for 5 minutes to cool slightly.

Stir the Cointreau into the sugar syrup and refrigerate for about an hour until cooled.

Combine the berries and cooled syrup in a large bowl and toss well. Spoon into a clean airtight container and store in the fridge for 24 hours to allow the flavours to infuse. Serve with whipped cream or spooned over vanilla ice cream.

Berries in liqueur syrup

Turkish Delight Ice Cream

Homemade ice cream may seem a little daunting to prepare, but this recipe will show you it isn't difficult at all, and may be adapted to suit any flavour variation you can think of. This ice cream is not suitable if you are lactose intolerant, or should be enjoyed in small quantities.

Serves 6–8
125 g caster sugar
5 egg yolks
1 teaspoon rosewater essence
2 drops red food colouring
200 ml thickened cream, lightly beaten
60 g dark chocolate, grated

Combine the sugar and 100 ml water in a small saucepan over low heat and stir until the sugar has dissolved. Increase the heat to medium and simmer rapidly for 10–15 minutes or until the syrup has reduced by half, stirring to ensure you don't burn the syrup.

Beat the egg yolks with electric beaters for 5–10 minutes until the mixture is thick, pale and creamy and has doubled in volume. Slowly pour the hot sugar syrup into the yolks and beat for a further 10 minutes, ensuring the mixture is well aerated and cooled.

Add the rosewater essence and food colouring to the cream and beat with electric beaters until just firm. Stir in the grated chocolate. Fold the cream mixture into the egg mixture, then pour into a 1-litre rectangular metal dish, cover with plastic film and freeze overnight.

Lemon Lime Ice Cream

This creamy ice cream has the subtle fragrance and flavour of lemon and lime, rather than an overpowering zesty tang. It is refreshing and indulgent at the same time. This ice cream is not suitable if you are lactose intolerant, or should be enjoyed in small quantities.

Serves 6–8
150 g caster sugar
grated zest of 1 small lemon, and a squeeze of lemon juice
grated zest of 1 lime, and a squeeze of lime juice
5 egg yolks
250 ml thickened cream, lightly beaten
thinly sliced preserved lemon rind, to serve

Combine the sugar, lemon and lime zest and 100 ml water in a small saucepan over low heat and stir until the sugar has dissolved. Increase the heat to medium and simmer rapidly for 10–15 minutes or until the syrup has reduced by half, stirring to ensure you don't burn the syrup.

Beat the egg yolks with electric beaters for 5–10 minutes until the mixture is thick, pale and creamy and has doubled in volume. Slowly pour the hot sugar syrup into the yolks and beat for a further 10 minutes, ensuring the mixture is well aerated and cooled. Fold in the cream and a squeeze of lemon and lime juice (add more to taste). Pour into a 1-litre rectangular metal dish, cover with plastic film and freeze overnight.

Serve decorated with slices of preserved lemon.

Lemon lime ice cream

*White chocolate panna cotta
with hazelnut sauce*

White Chocolate Panna Cotta with Hazelnut Sauce

My sister Linda can never go past panna cotta. Since giving her this recipe, I've noticed it features at her home-cooked dinners alarmingly often! This is not suitable for the lactose intolerant.

Serves 4
1 cup cream
1 cup milk
2 teaspoons vanilla bean paste
    or 1 tablespoon vanilla extract
⅓ cup caster sugar
50 g white chocolate, grated
3 tablespoons boiling water
1 tablespoon powdered gelatine

Hazelnut sauce
⅓ cup brown sugar
2 tablespoons cocoa powder, sifted
1¼ tablespoons gluten-free cornflour
1½ cups milk
2 tablespoons hazelnut liqueur

Heat the cream, milk, vanilla, sugar and chocolate in a saucepan over low heat. Stir occasionally until the chocolate has melted.

Combine the boiling water and gelatine in a small heatproof bowl. Set the bowl over a larger bowl of boiling water, stirring constantly until the gelatine has dissolved. Stir the dissolved gelatine into the chocolate mixture. Pour into four 150 ml panna cotta moulds and refrigerate for 3–4 hours or overnight until set.

To make the sauce, combine the sugar, cocoa powder and cornflour in a small saucepan. Stir in a little milk to form a paste, then add the remaining milk and mix well to ensure there are no lumps. Stir over medium–high heat until the sauce has thickened slightly, then remove from the heat and stir in the hazelnut liqueur. Transfer to a jug, cover and refrigerate until ready to serve, poured over the panna cotta.

Pancakes with Strawberry Coulis

While debittered soy flour is recommended in all recipes using soy flour in this book, it is not essential, as the bitter soy taste does disappear when cooked. It just means that licking the bowl does not taste so good!

Makes 6–8
120 g fine rice flour
20 g debittered soy flour
50 g gluten-free cornflour
¾ teaspoon bicarbonate of soda
2½ tablespoons sugar
1 egg, lightly beaten
150 ml low-fat milk
40 g butter, melted
non-stick cooking spray

Strawberry coulis
250 g strawberries, hulled
juice of 1 lemon
½ cup caster sugar

Sift the flours and bicarbonate of soda three times into a bowl (or mix well with a whisk to ensure they are well combined), then add the sugar. Whisk together the beaten egg and milk in a bowl, pour into the dry ingredients and mix with a spoon until well combined. Stir in the melted butter and set aside for 10 minutes.

To make the strawberry coulis, place all the ingredients in a food processor and blend until the sugar has dissolved and the puree is smooth and glossy. Strain through a fine sieve and discard the seeds.

Heat a frying pan over low–medium heat for 2 minutes. Spray with non-stick spray, then add 3–4 tablespoons batter for each pancake. Cook for 2–3 minutes until bubbles start to appear, then flip over and cook for 2 minutes. Remove from the pan and keep warm while you make the remaining pancakes. Serve with the strawberry coulis.

Caramel Banana Tart

Sheets of ready-rolled gluten-free shortcrust pastry are now available from larger health-food stores with freezer facilities, and can also be ordered from on-line stockists or manufacturers.

Serves 10–12
30 cm square sheet ready-made gluten-free
   sweet shortcrust pastry
whipped cream, to serve

Banana filling
385 ml tin sweetened condensed milk
250 g cream cheese
1 tablespoon lemon juice
3 ripe bananas

Caramel base
½ cup cream
½ cup brown sugar
1 tablespoon gluten-free cornflour
15 g butter

Preheat the oven to 170°C and grease a 23 cm fluted tart dish.

Ease the pastry into the tart dish and trim the edges. Bake for 10 minutes or until golden brown. Set aside to cool completely.

For the filling, place the condensed milk, cream cheese, lemon juice and two of the bananas in a food processor, and process for about 2 minutes or until evenly combined.

To make the caramel base, place the cream, brown sugar and cornflour in a small saucepan and stir well to remove any lumps. Heat over medium heat, stirring until the mixture is thick and smooth. Turn off heat and stir in the butter until fully melted.

Slice the remaining banana into 2 mm thick slices and place evenly over the pastry base. Pour the caramel over the banana and spread with a metal spoon until the banana slices are evenly covered. Pour the banana filling over the caramel bananas.

Bake for 30–40 minutes or until firm to touch and lightly golden. Remove from the oven and cool to room temperature, then refrigerate for 3 hours. Top with whipped cream and serve.

Choc Mint Mousse

The combination of mint and chocolate in this smooth, rich mousse makes it a divine indulgence. Try your hardest to limit yourself to a small serve, especially if you are lactose intolerant.

Serves 4
3 tablespoons boiling water
1½ teaspoons powdered gelatine
200 g good-quality dark cooking chocolate
150 ml thickened cream, plus extra to serve
1½ teaspoons peppermint essence
3 eggs, separated
2 tablespoons caster sugar
cocoa powder, for dusting (optional)
gluten-free after-dinner mints, to serve

Combine the boiling water and gelatine in a small heatproof bowl. Set the bowl over a larger bowl of boiling water, stirring constantly until the gelatine has dissolved.

Combine the chocolate, cream and peppermint essence in a heatproof bowl. Place the bowl over a saucepan of simmering water, ensuring the base doesn't touch the water, and stir until melted. Cool to room temperature, then stir in the dissolved gelatine and egg yolks, one at a time.

Place the egg whites in small clean bowl and beat with electric beaters until soft peaks form. Add the sugar and beat until dissolved.

Using a large metal spoon, gently fold the egg whites into the chocolate mixture in two batches. Pour the mixture into four ⅔ cup serving dishes and refrigerate for 3–4 hours or overnight. Dust with cocoa powder if you like, and serve with gluten-free after-dinner mints.

Choc mint mousse

Vanilla Sago Puddings

Sago desserts are almost too easy to make! This one is lactose- and dairy-free, but it's so creamy you'd never know it.

Serves 6
1 litre gluten-free soy milk
½ cup caster sugar
3 teaspoons vanilla bean paste
    or 1½ tablespoons vanilla essence
⅔ cup sago

Combine the milk, sugar and vanilla in a medium saucepan over high heat and gradually bring to a simmer. Stir the sago into the milk and simmer over low heat for 20–25 minutes, stirring regularly, until the sago resembles translucent jelly-like balls. Remove from the heat and set aside to cool for 20 minutes.

Stir to remove any skin set on top, then pour evenly into six glass serving bowls. Cover and place in the refrigerator for 3–4 hours or overnight.

Brandy Snaps with Vanilla Cream Filling

While they are still warm, you can also shape the snaps into baskets that can be filled with a scoop of ice cream and topped with fresh fruit.

Makes 24
100 g unsalted butter
⅔ cup brown sugar
⅓ cup golden syrup
65 g fine rice flour
2 teaspoons ground ginger

Vanilla cream
600 ml thickened cream
½ cup pure icing sugar
1 teaspoon vanilla essence

Preheat the oven to 180°C. Line two baking trays with baking paper.

Combine the butter, sugar and syrup in a small saucepan over medium heat and stir until the sugar has dissolved. Remove from the heat. Sift the flour and ginger into the pan and stir until well combined. Cover and keep warm.

You will need to make the snaps in batches of two or three per tray as they will need room to spread. Drop 1–2 teaspoons of mixture onto the baking trays and bake for 7–8 minutes until golden brown and bubbles have formed. They should be quite dark – if they are too light, the brandy snap will not become crisp and set properly.

Cool the snaps for 1–2 minutes, then carefully lift from the trays and wrap around a cone mould or thin rolling pin. Cool slightly, then slide off the mould. Cool completely, then store in an airtight container.

To make the vanilla cream, beat the cream, icing sugar and vanilla essence until thick. Refrigerate until needed.

When ready, pipe the cream mixture into the brandy snaps and serve immediately. The snaps become soggy if filled too early.

Brandy snaps with vanilla cream filling

Baked Custard with Maple Syrup

The silky-textured custard contrasts beautifully with the lingering flavour of maple syrup in this dessert, which can be served warm or cold.

Preheat the oven to 180°C and grease a 23 cm round baking dish.

Beat the eggs, sugar and vanilla essence in a bowl. Gradually add the hot milk, stirring well to combine.

Pour the mixture into the baking dish. Put the dish in a deep roasting tin and pour hot water into the tin to a depth of 2.5 cm. Bake for 15–20 minutes, or until the centre is firm when shaken. Pour the maple syrup over the top while still hot and serve.

Serves 4
2 eggs, lightly beaten
⅓ cup caster sugar
1 teaspoon vanilla essence
2 cups low-fat milk, heated
    (use lactose-free milk if
    lactose intolerant)
½ cup maple syrup

Chocolate Rice Pudding

Like a good risotto, this rice dessert does take a while to prepare, but I am sure you will agree it is worth the wait. Add a tablespoon or two of flavoured liqueur for a great flavour twist.

Serves 4

1 litre low-fat milk (use lactose-free milk
    if lactose intolerant)
½ cup medium-grain white rice
⅓ cup caster sugar
150 g good-quality dark chocolate, broken into pieces
2 tablespoons coffee or coconut liqueur (optional)

Combine all the ingredients (except the liqueur) in a medium saucepan and cook over medium–high heat, stirring constantly, until the mixture comes to the boil. Reduce the heat to medium and cook, stirring regularly, for about 40–45 minutes until thick and creamy and the rice is tender. Remove from the heat and add the liqueur if using. Spoon into individual serving dishes. Serve warm or refrigerate for 3–4 hours before serving.

Orange and Poppy-seed Souffles

Souffles can often seem daunting, but they are not difficult at all. These light desserts are always a hit with guests.

Serves 6

butter, for greasing
120 g caster sugar, plus extra for coating
3 tablespoons gluten-free cornflour
1 cup milk
3 egg yolks
grated zest and juice of 1 orange
2 teaspoons poppy seeds
50 g caster sugar, extra
5 egg whites

Preheat the oven to 200°C. Grease six 1-cup souffle dishes with butter, and coat with caster sugar.

Combine the cornflour with 1 tablespoon milk and 1 egg yolk in a small bowl.

Heat the remaining milk, orange zest and juice in a small saucepan over medium heat until the mixture boils (the mixture will appear curdled, but this is fine). Remove from the heat and stir in the cornflour mix until well combined. Return to the stovetop and cook over low heat until the custard thickens, stirring constantly.

In a small bowl, mix together the poppy seeds, 50 g sugar and the remaining egg yolks until well combined. Add to the orange custard and cook for 2–3 minutes, stirring constantly. Transfer to a large bowl and allow to cool slightly.

In a large bowl, beat the egg whites until stiff peaks form. Add the remaining sugar and beat until dissolved. Fold half the egg whites into the orange custard, then fold in the rest.

Spoon the mixture into the souffle dishes, filling them to about 1 cm from the top, and level with a spatula. Bake for about 12–15 minutes or until risen. Serve immediately.

Orange and poppy-seed souffles

Pumpkin Pie

Although it may sound strange to some, this recipe is in the correct section of this cookbook! This vegetable-based dish makes a fantastic dessert.

Serves 10
130 g fine rice flour
75 g gluten-free cornflour
45 g debittered soy flour
1 teaspoon xanthan gum (optional)
160 g butter
120 ml iced water

Pumpkin filling
3 eggs
½ cup lightly packed brown sugar
2 tablespoons maple syrup
1½ cups mashed pumpkin
¾ cup light cream
1 teaspoon ground cinnamon
1 teaspoon ground ginger

Sift the flours and xanthan gum (if using) three times into a bowl (or mix well with a whisk to ensure they are well combined). Combine the flours and butter in a food processor until the mixture resembles fine breadcrumbs. Continue processing, adding 1 tablespoon iced water at a time, until a soft dough forms. Turn out onto a gluten-free floured board and knead for 2–3 minutes or until smooth. Wrap in plastic film and refrigerate for 30 minutes.

Grease a 22 cm pie dish. Roll out the pastry between two sheets of baking paper to a thickness of 3–5 mm. Ease into the pie dish and trim the edges. Cover and refrigerate for 30 minutes.

Preheat the oven to 200°C.

Line the pastry case with baking paper, fill with baking beads or rice and blind-bake for 10–15 minutes or until golden brown. Remove the baking beads and cook for a further 10–12 minutes or until golden brown. Remove from the oven and set aside to cool. Reduce the temperature to 150°C.

To make the filling, beat the eggs, brown sugar, maple syrup, pumpkin, cream and spices with electric beaters for 1–2 minutes until well combined.

Pour the filling into the cooled pastry case and bake for 30 minutes, then cover with foil and bake for a further 20–30 minutes until the filling is firm to touch. Serve with whipped cream or ice cream or both!

Cappuccino Creme Brulee

This classic dessert is just delicious with the addition of a cappuccino flavour. A kitchen blowtorch is ideal to make the toffee, but you can also caramelise the sugar under the grill or use a hot metal spoon (see below).

Serves 4
600 ml cream
1 teaspoon vanilla essence
8 egg yolks
¾ cup brown sugar
3–4 teaspoons instant coffee
1 tablespoon boiling water
1 tablespoon coffee liqueur (optional)
⅓ cup caster sugar

Combine the cream and vanilla essence in a small saucepan and heat gently over low heat until the mixture just comes to the boil. Remove from the heat and cool slightly.

Place the egg yolks and brown sugar in a small bowl and beat with electric beaters until thick, pale and creamy. Pour the vanilla cream over the egg mixture and whisk to combine. Return to the saucepan and stir over low heat for 6–8 minutes or until the mixture has thickened enough to coat the back of a spoon.

In a small bowl, dissolve the instant coffee in the boiling water. Add the liqueur (if using) and stir into the egg mixture. Pour the egg mixture into a glass bowl set over a larger bowl of ice to stop the cooking process.

Pour the custard evenly into four ¾ cup ramekins, then refrigerate for 3 hours or until set.

When ready to serve, sprinkle each brulee with 1 tablespoon caster sugar. Using an oven mitt, hold a metal spoon over an open flame until very hot. Run the hot spoon over the sugar so it melts and caramelises. Alternatively, use a blowtorch or melt the sugar under a warm grill.

Rich Mocha Truffles

As the name indicates, these truffles are indeed rich. Make sure you use good-quality dark chocolate to make the decadent experience complete.

Makes about 30
375 g dark chocolate, chopped
⅓ cup thickened cream
⅓ cup coffee liqueur
cocoa powder, for dusting

Place the chocolate, cream and liqueur in a medium glass bowl. Set the bowl over a saucepan of simmering water (make sure the base of the bowl does not touch the water) and stir until the chocolate has melted and the mixture is smooth. Remove from the heat, and chill in the fridge for 2 hours until the mixture is firm enough to roll into balls.

Line a baking tray with baking paper and sift the cocoa onto a plate.

Roll 1–2 teaspoons of the chocolate mixture into balls that are 2–3 cm in diameter, then roll in the cocoa powder until well coated (do this in batches of five or six truffles). Place the truffles on the lined tray and repeat with the remaining chocolate mixture and cocoa. Refrigerate for 1 hour prior to serving.

Rich mocha truffles

Four puddings

Offer me a generous helping of steamed pudding with
homemade custard and I'm a very happy girl. Turn the page
for four scrumptious recipes that you will find hard to resist.

Steamed Butterscotch Puddings

Makes 4

70 g butter
1 cup brown sugar
1 egg, beaten
100 g fine rice flour
35 g gluten-free cornflour
30 g tapioca flour
2 teaspoons gluten-free baking powder
½ teaspoon bicarbonate of soda
1 teaspoon xanthan gum (optional)
3 tablespoons milk

Butterscotch sauce
½ cup cream
100 g brown sugar
20 g butter

Grease four 1 cup ramekins.

Place the butter and sugar in a medium bowl and beat with electric beaters until pale and creamy. Add the egg and combine well. Sift the flours, baking powder, bicarbonate of soda and xanthan gum (if using) three times into a bowl (or mix well with a whisk to ensure they are well combined). Add the flour mixture and milk to the butter mixture and beat until just combined. Spoon the batter into the ramekins.

Cut four 15 cm square pieces of baking paper and secure over the ramekins with elastic bands. Place in a large saucepan and pour enough boiling water into the pan to reach two-thirds of the way up the sides of the ramekins. Cover and cook over medium heat for 20–25 minutes, or until a skewer comes out clean.

Meanwhile, to make the sauce, combine all the ingredients in a saucepan over medium heat. Stir constantly until the sugar has dissolved and the sauce has thickened slightly.

Turn out the puddings onto serving plates and drizzle with the warm butterscotch sauce.

Chocolate Rocky Road Self-saucing Pudding

Serves 6–8

85 g fine rice flour
65 g tapioca flour
2 tablespoons debittered soy flour
3 tablespoons caster sugar
2 tablespoons cocoa powder
2 teaspoons gluten-free baking powder
90 g dark chocolate, chopped
40 g red gluten-free jelly confectionery, chopped
½ cup milk
40 g unsalted butter, melted
1 egg, lightly beaten
½ teaspoon vanilla essence
50 g gluten-free marshmallows, chopped

Chocolate sauce
150 g brown sugar
2 tablespoons cocoa powder
1 cup boiling water

Preheat the oven to 180°C and grease a 1.25 litre pudding basin.

Sift the flours, sugar, cocoa and baking powder into a bowl. Stir in the chocolate and gluten-free jelly confectionery.

Combine the milk, melted butter, egg and vanilla in a small jug. Add to the dry ingredients and mix well, then pour the batter into the pudding basin.

To make the sauce, mix together all the ingredients in a jug and carefully pour over the batter. Bake for 35–45 minutes or until firm in the centre.

To serve, spoon the hot pudding and its sauce into bowls and sprinkle with the chopped marshmallows.

Bread and Butter Pudding

Serves 6–8

8–10 slices white gluten-free bread
25 g butter, softened
2 ripe bananas, sliced
3 tablespoons sultanas
2 eggs
2 cups low-fat milk
1 teaspoon vanilla essence
2 tablespoons brown sugar
3 tablespoons raspberry jam
ice cream, to serve

Preheat the oven to 160°C and lightly grease a 20 cm × 20 cm baking dish.

Lightly spread the bread slices with butter and cut each slice into triangles or small squares. Layer in the baking dish with the sliced banana and sultanas.

Whisk together the eggs, milk, vanilla essence and brown sugar and pour over the bread. Set aside for 15 minutes so the bread absorbs the liquid.

Spoon small amounts of raspberry jam over the top and bake for 40–45 minutes until golden brown and the custard has set. Serve warm with ice cream. Recipe pictured on pages 114 and 115.

Christmas Pudding

Serves 10–12

1 cup sultanas
¾ cup raisins
½ cup craisins (dried cranberries)
1 cup glace cherries, chopped
½ cup brandy
65 g fine rice flour
35 g gluten-free cornflour
20 g debittered soy flour
60 g butter
1 cup brown sugar
2 cups fresh gluten-free breadcrumbs
1 teaspoon mixed spice
3 eggs
½ cup low-fat milk

Grease a 1 litre pudding basin and line with baking paper.

Place the dried fruit in a large mixing bowl, add the brandy and mix well. Cover and refrigerate overnight.

Sift the flours three times into a bowl (or mix well with a whisk to ensure they are well combined). Rub in the butter until the mixture resembles fine breadcrumbs. Add the soaked fruit, sugar, breadcrumbs and mixed spice.

In a small mixing bowl, lightly beat the eggs and milk. Pour over the fruit mixture and mix to combine.

Pour the mixture into the pudding basin, then place the basin in a large stockpot. Pour enough water into the stockpot to come three-quarters of the way up the side of the pudding basin. Bring the water to the boil, then reduce to a gentle simmer and cook the pudding for 2–3 hours. Check the water regularly to ensure it does not run dry. If making ahead, the pudding may be resteamed for 1 hour on the day of serving.

Baking

rice flour

amaranth flour

millet flour

RECIPE INDEX

polenta

xanthum gum

Strawberry and Cream Cakes

These simple cakes are just delicious. I make them big because there is absolutely no point in doing things by halves for a treat that tastes this good!

Preheat the oven to 180°C. Line a six-hole large muffin tin with patty cases.

Place the butter, sugar and vanilla essence in a medium bowl and beat with electric beaters for 2–3 minutes until pale and creamy. Add the eggs, one at a time, beating well between additions.

Sift the flours, bicarbonate of soda, baking powder and xanthan gum (if using) three times into a bowl (or mix well with a whisk to ensure they are well combined). Gradually add to the creamed butter mixture, stirring to combine. Fold in the cream and strawberries.

Spoon the batter into the muffin holes until about three-quarters full and smooth the tops. Bake for 20–25 minutes or until golden brown and firm to touch. Remove from the oven and leave in the tin for 5 minutes, then transfer to a wire rack to cool. Dust with icing sugar before serving.

Makes 6
100 g butter, softened
⅔ cup caster sugar
2 teaspoons vanilla essence
2 eggs, at room temperature
100 g fine rice flour
35 g gluten-free cornflour
20 g debittered soy flour
1 teaspoon bicarbonate of soda
2 teaspoons gluten-free baking powder
1 teaspoon xanthan gum (optional)
½ cup light cream
250 g strawberries, hulled and diced
pure icing sugar, for dusting

Moist Family Chocolate Cake

We all need a basic chocolate cake recipe that works. This is my old faithful –
I know it will work beautifully every time.

Serves 10–12
170 g fine rice flour
75 g gluten-free cornflour
90 g potato flour
70 g cocoa powder
2 teaspoons gluten-free baking powder
1 teaspoon bicarbonate of soda
1 teaspoon xanthan gum (optional)
2 eggs
330 g sugar
50 g unsalted butter, melted
200 g gluten-free vanilla yoghurt
⅔ cup low-fat milk

Chocolate frosting
1½ cups pure icing sugar
2–3 tablespoons cocoa powder
100 g unsalted butter, at room
    temperature
3 tablespoons milk

Preheat the oven to 170°C and grease a 23 cm springform cake tin.

Sift the flours, cocoa, baking powder, bicarbonate of soda and xanthan gum (if using) three times into a bowl (or mix well with a whisk to ensure they are well combined).

Whisk the eggs and sugar until thick and foamy. Add the melted butter, yoghurt and milk and stir until well combined. Add to the dry ingredients and beat with electric beaters for 2–3 minutes.

Pour the batter into the tin and bake for 35–40 minutes or until firm to touch (a skewer inserted into the centre of the cake should come out clean). Leave in the tin for 5 minutes, then turn out onto a wire rack to cool completely.

To make the chocolate frosting, sift the icing sugar and cocoa powder into a bowl. Add the butter and milk and mix until well combined. Spread evenly over the cooled cake.

Lime and Coconut Muffins

The kiwi fruit may seem to be an unusual addition to this recipe, but it adds a wonderful moisture to these delightful muffins.

Makes 12

60 g butter, softened
¾ cup low-fat milk
2 eggs, at room temperature
2 teaspoons vanilla essence
1 cup caster sugar
170 g fine rice flour
75 g gluten-free cornflour
90 g buckwheat flour
1 teaspoon bicarbonate of soda
2 teaspoons gluten-free baking powder
1 teaspoon xanthan gum (optional)
1 tablespoon grated lime zest
2 kiwi fruit, roughly chopped
3 tablespoons shredded coconut

Preheat the oven to 170°C. Line a 12-hole standard muffin tin with patty cases.

Whisk together the butter, milk, eggs, vanilla essence and sugar in a jug.

Sift the flours, bicarbonate of soda, baking powder and xanthan gum (if using) three times into a bowl (or mix well with a whisk to ensure they are well combined). Add the lime zest and kiwi fruit and mix together well. Make a well in the centre and pour in the egg mixture. Stir until just combined, then spoon the mixture into the muffin holes and top with shredded coconut. Bake for 20 minutes or until firm to touch. Leave in the tin for 5 minutes, then transfer to a wire rack to cool.

Lemon and Blueberry Friands

The flavour combination of lemon and blueberry in these miniature almond cakes is a delightful taste sensation.

Makes 8

140 g unsalted butter

1½ cups pure icing sugar

35 g gluten-free cornflour

45 g fine rice flour

1¼ cups ground almonds

5 egg whites, lightly whisked

1 tablespoon grated lemon zest

1 tablespoon lemon juice

1 teaspoon vanilla essence

200 g blueberries (tinned or fresh)

Preheat the oven to 180°C and lightly grease eight friand tins.

Melt the butter in a small saucepan over low heat, then cook for a further 3–4 minutes until brown flecks appear. Remove from the heat.

Sift the icing sugar and flours three times into a bowl and stir in the ground almonds. Add the egg whites, lemon zest, lemon juice, vanilla essence and melted butter and stir with a metal spoon until well combined.

Spoon the mixture into the friand tins until two-thirds full and sprinkle a few blueberries on top. Bake for 12–15 minutes until light golden and firm to touch (a skewer inserted into the centre should come out clean). Allow to stand in the tin for 5 minutes before transferring to a wire rack to cool.

Pumpkin Loaf

This loaf is not savoury, but is not overly sweet either, making it the perfect treat for any time of the day.

Serves 10–12

125 g butter, at room temperature, cubed
¾ cup brown sugar
2 eggs
400 g mashed pumpkin
3 tablespoons milk
140 g rice flour
75 g gluten-free cornflour
45 g debittered soy flour
2 tablespoons instant polenta
1 teaspoon ground cinnamon
2 teaspoons gluten-free baking powder
1 teaspoon bicarbonate of soda
1 teaspoon xanthan gum (optional)

Preheat the oven to 170°C. Grease and line a 9 cm × 19 cm loaf tin.

Place the butter and brown sugar in a large bowl and beat with electric beaters until thick and creamy. Add the eggs, one at a time, beating well between additions. Add the pumpkin and milk and beat until just combined.

Sift the flours, polenta, cinnamon, baking powder, bicarbonate of soda and xanthan gum (if using) three times into a bowl (or mix well with a whisk to ensure they are well combined). Fold the dry ingredients into the pumpkin mixture with a large metal spoon until just combined.

Spoon the mixture into the loaf tin and bake for 45 minutes. Cover with foil and bake for a further 15 minutes or until a skewer inserted into the centre comes out clean. Cool in the tin for 15–20 minutes before turning out onto a wire rack.

Melting Moments

I have suggested using a commercially prepared gluten-free flour in this recipe – they work well in biscuit recipes and are readily available these days. However, an alternative would be to replace the plain gluten-free flour with ⅔ cup fine rice flour and ⅓ cup tapioca flour.

Makes 15

½ cup pure icing sugar, sifted
200 g unsalted butter, at room
    temperature, cubed
½ teaspoon vanilla essence
1 tablespoon finely grated orange zest
1 cup gluten-free custard powder
1 cup gluten-free plain flour

Passionfruit cream

30 g unsalted butter, at room
    temperature, cubed
1 cup pure icing sugar, sifted
2 tablespoons fresh passionfruit pulp

Preheat the oven to 180°C and line two baking trays with baking paper.

Place the icing sugar, butter, vanilla essence and orange zest in a medium bowl and beat with electric beaters until well combined.

Sift the custard powder and flour into a bowl. Add to the creamed butter and mix to form a firm dough. Use your hands when the mixture becomes too stiff to mix with the spoon.

Roll the dough into 30 small balls, place on the baking trays and press with a fork. Bake for 10–15 minutes or until lightly browned on the base. Remove from the oven and leave on the trays for 5 minutes before transferring to wire racks to cool completely.

To make the passionfruit cream, mix the butter and ½ cup icing sugar in a small bowl with a metal spoon until pale and creamy. Add the remaining icing sugar and passionfruit pulp and beat until thick and pale.

Spread the passionfruit cream on the base of half the biscuits and sandwich together with the remaining biscuits.

Basic Sponge

I have to thank my Nana for this recipe. I have provided various topping suggestions, but my favourite will always be passionfruit icing – just the way Nana used to make it for me.

Serves 10
150 g gluten-free cornflour
1 teaspoon cream of tartar
½ teaspoon bicarbonate of soda
4 eggs, at room temperature
¾ cup caster sugar
whipped cream, to serve

Preheat the oven to 170°C. Grease two 20 cm sponge tins and line with baking paper.

Sift the flour, cream of tartar and bicarbonate of soda three times into a bowl.

Place the eggs and sugar in a medium bowl and beat with electric beaters for 8–10 minutes or until tripled in volume. Fold the flour mixture into the egg mixture until just combined – do not overmix.

Pour the batter evenly into the sponge tins and bake for 15–20 minutes or until the mixture starts to come away from the edge of the tin. Cool the cakes in the tins for 5–10 minutes before turning out onto a wire rack to cool completely.

Fill the sponge with whipped cream and top with whatever you like: strawberries, crushed nuts, gluten-free toffee pieces or passionfruit cream (see page 130).

Banana Hazelnut Cake

The unexpected ingredient in this recipe is the mashed potato. Don't be alarmed – the finished result is delicious. Now I bet you can't wait to get to the kitchen and see for yourself!

Serves 12
4 eggs, separated
2 teaspoons vanilla essence
1 teaspoon gluten-free baking powder
½ teaspoon bicarbonate of soda
180 g caster sugar
40 g butter, at room temperature
1 teaspoon ground cinnamon
150 g cooled smoothly mashed potato
2 medium ripe bananas, mashed
1½ cups ground hazelnuts
½ cup chopped walnuts (optional)
pure icing sugar, for dusting (optional)

Preheat the oven to 180°C. Grease and line a 24 cm springform cake tin.

Place the egg whites, vanilla, baking powder and bicarbonate of soda in a large bowl and beat with electric beaters until firm peaks form.

Beat the egg yolks, sugar, butter and cinnamon until thick, pale and creamy. In a separate bowl, combine the mashed potato, banana, hazelnut meal and walnuts (if using).

Fold alternate batches of egg white and mashed potato mix into the egg yolk mixture. Spoon the cake batter into the tin and bake for 20 minutes, then cover with foil and cook for a further 10–15 minutes or until a skewer inserted into the centre comes out clean. Serve dusted with icing sugar, if desired.

Banana hazelnut cake

Fruit, Nut and Seed Cake

This is a heavy cake, high in fibre and chock-a-block full of flavour and goodness. A little goes a long way.

Preheat the oven to 160°C. Grease a 20 cm springform cake tin and line with baking paper.

Combine the sultanas, raisins, pineapple, cinnamon, nutmeg, cloves, butter, sugar and 1¼ cups water in a medium saucepan over medium heat. Stir until the sugar has dissolved, then increase the heat and bring to the boil. Boil for 1 minute, then reduce the heat and simmer for 2–3 minutes. Transfer to a large bowl and cool to room temperature.

Sift the flours, baking powder, bicarbonate of soda and xanthan gum (if using) three times into a bowl (or mix well with a whisk to ensure they are well combined).

Add the egg, pecans, sunflower seeds and pumpkin seeds to the fruit mixture, then stir in the sifted flour mixture. Pour into the cake tin and sprinkle the extra pumpkin and sunflower seeds on top. Cover with foil and bake for 50 minutes, then remove the foil and bake for a further 20 minutes or until a skewer inserted into the centre of the cake comes out clean.

Serves 10

½ cup sultanas
½ cup raisins
½ cup chopped glace pineapple
1 teaspoon ground cinnamon
½ teaspoon ground nutmeg
½ teaspoon ground cloves
30 g butter
½ cup caster sugar
140 g brown rice flour
90 g buckwheat flour
2 teaspoons gluten-free baking powder
1 teaspoon bicarbonate of soda
1 teaspoon xanthan gum (optional)
3 eggs, lightly beaten
¾ cup chopped pecans
½ cup sunflower seeds
½ cup pumpkin seeds
3 tablespoons pumpkin seeds, extra
3 tablespoons sunflower seeds, extra

Choc Rough Nut Slice

This slice is so easy to make, and it's a real crowd-pleaser. I like to add the rum for a subtle flavour twist, but it is optional.

Makes about 25 pieces
200 g dark chocolate
50 g butter
½ cup peanuts
½ cup desiccated coconut
½ cup sultanas
⅓ cup sweetened condensed milk
2 tablespoons dark rum (optional)

Line an 18 cm square baking tin with baking paper.

Melt the chocolate and butter in a small saucepan over medium heat. Remove from the heat and set aside to cool slightly. Stir in the nuts, coconut, sultanas, condensed milk and rum (if using).

Spoon the mixture into the lined tin and refrigerate until firm. Cut into small slices to serve.

Muesli Biscuits

These more-ish biscuits have a similar taste and texture to Anzac biscuits, with a hint of golden syrup in every bite. For those with fructose malabsorption, choose a muesli with a low dried-fruit content.

Preheat the oven to 160°C and line two baking trays with baking paper.

Combine the muesli, flours, coconut and sugar in a large bowl.

In a small mixing bowl, dissolve the bicarbonate of soda in the boiling water. Add the melted butter and golden syrup and mix until well combined. Pour into the dry ingredients and mix well. You may need to add more fine rice flour – the amount required will vary according to the type of muesli used. The mixture should be firm enough to form round balls.

Shape teaspoons of the mixture into balls and place on the baking trays, leaving room for spreading. Press with a fork to flatten slightly, then bake for 10–12 minutes or until golden brown. Remove from the oven and cool on the trays for 10 minutes before transferring to a wire rack to cool completely.

Makes about 35
1 cup gluten-free muesli
90 g fine rice flour
90 g tapioca flour
¾ cup desiccated coconut
½ cup caster sugar
½ teaspoon bicarbonate of soda
3 tablespoons boiling water
125 g butter, melted
2 tablespoons golden syrup, warmed

Ginger and Date Slice

This one is for my dad, who loves ginger in any recipe. For those on a low-FODMAP™ diet (see page 3), leave out the dates and double the ginger.

Makes about 30 pieces
200 ml sweetened condensed milk
¾ cup lightly packed brown sugar
125 g butter
60 g dates, pitted and chopped
60 g crystallised ginger, finely chopped
1 teaspoon ground ginger
250 g plain sweet gluten-free biscuits, crushed
100 g dark chocolate

Grease a 20 cm square baking dish and line with baking paper.

Place the condensed milk, brown sugar and butter in a small saucepan over medium heat and stir until the sugar has dissolved. Add the dates, crystallised ginger, ground ginger and crushed biscuits and mix with a metal spoon until well combined. Press into the baking dish and smooth the surface.

Break the chocolate into pieces and place in a heatproof bowl. Set the bowl over a saucepan of simmering water, ensuring the base doesn't touch the water, and stir until melted.

Drizzle the melted chocolate over the slice, then cool in the refrigerator for 2 hours. Cut into slices to serve.

Almond and Brazil Nut Slice

The almond essence gives the slice a subtle marzipan flavour, which I find delicious. However, if you consider this flavour a little overpowering, just leave it out.

Makes about 30 pieces
½ cup slivered almonds
½ cup chopped brazil nuts
150 g plain sweet gluten-free biscuits, crushed
⅓ cup caster sugar
½ cup desiccated coconut
125 g butter, melted
1 teaspoon almond essence

Preheat the oven to 180°C and line a baking tray with baking paper. Lightly grease a 15 cm square baking dish and line with baking paper.

Spread out the almonds and brazil nuts on the lined tray and bake for 5 minutes or until they are just starting to turn golden brown. Set aside 2 tablespoons of the toasted almonds and place the rest of the nuts in a large bowl.

Add the crushed biscuits, sugar and coconut to the nuts. Stir in the melted butter and almond essence and mix together with a metal spoon.

Spoon the mixture into the baking dish and smooth the surface. Sprinkle the reserved almonds over the top and press gently into the slice. Refrigerate for 3 hours or until firm. Turn out of the baking dish and cut into fingers to serve.

Almond and brazil nut slice

Afghan Biscuits

This is a gluten-free variation of another old-time favourite. Just make sure you buy gluten-free cornflakes – many brands use malt as an ingredient.

Makes 30

1 cup brown sugar

190 g unsalted butter, at room
    temperature

100 g fine rice flour

65 g tapioca flour

1 teaspoon bicarbonate of soda

2 teaspoons gluten-free baking powder

2 tablespoons cocoa powder

1½ cups gluten-free cornflakes

Chocolate icing

1½ cups pure icing sugar

1½ tablespoons cocoa powder

Preheat the oven to 180°C and line two baking trays with baking paper.

Place the sugar and butter in a large bowl and beat with electric beaters on medium speed for 2–3 minutes or until light and fluffy.

Sift the flours, bicarbonate of soda, baking powder and cocoa powder three times into a bowl (or mix well with a whisk to ensure they are well combined). Add to the creamed butter and beat well. Gently stir in the cornflakes.

Roll the mixture into walnut-sized balls and flatten slightly by pressing gently between your palms. Place on the baking trays, allowing room for spreading, and bake for 8–10 minutes or until golden. Cool for 10 minutes on the baking trays, then transfer to a wire rack to cool completely.

To make the chocolate icing, sift the cocoa powder and icing sugar into a small bowl. Add 1½–2 tablespoons water and mix until smooth. Drizzle the icing over the cooled biscuits and leave to set.

Butterfly Cupcakes

I love making these with my niece Zoe and nephew Joel. We have a great time filling the holes with cream and placing the wings on top. But the best fun, of course, is in the eating.

Makes 12

150 g butter, at room temperature
150 g caster sugar
2 teaspoons vanilla essence
2 eggs, lightly beaten
100 g fine rice flour
50 g gluten-free cornflour
40 g tapioca flour
1 teaspoon bicarbonate of soda
2 teaspoons gluten-free baking powder
1 teaspoon xanthan gum (optional)
¾ cup sour cream
1 cup whipped cream
icing sugar, for dusting

Preheat the oven to 170°C and line a 12-hole muffin tin with patty cases.

Beat the butter, sugar and vanilla essence with electric beaters until pale and creamy. Add the eggs, one at a time, beating well between additions.

Sift the flours, bicarbonate of soda, baking powder and xanthan gum (if using) three times into a bowl (or mix well with a whisk to ensure they are well combined). Fold the dry ingredients into the butter mixture in batches, alternating with the sour cream.

Spoon the mixture into the patty cases and bake for 12–15 minutes or until golden brown and firm to touch. Cool in the tin for 5 minutes, then transfer to a wire rack to cool completely.

Using a small sharp-pointed knife, cut a small circle from the top of each cupcake and cut in half to make 'wings'. Fill the hole with whipped cream, then arrange the cut halves in the cream to resemble wings. Dust with icing sugar just before serving.

Coffee and Pecan Cake

This is a lovely moist cake with a subtle coffee flavour. I often make it when I know friends will be dropping in for afternoon tea.

Serves 10–12

1½ tablespoons instant coffee
2 teaspoons boiling water
160 g butter, at room temperature
1 cup caster sugar
3 eggs
130 g fine rice flour
35 g gluten-free cornflour
30 g tapioca flour
1 teaspoon bicarbonate of soda
2 teaspoons gluten-free baking powder
1 teaspoon xanthan gum (optional)
½ cup sour cream
pure icing sugar, for dusting

Pecan topping

40 g butter, at room temperature, cubed
½ cup brown sugar
1½ teaspoons ground cinnamon
2 teaspoons instant coffee
1 cup pecans, roughly chopped

Preheat the oven to 180°C. Grease a 20 cm square baking tin and line with baking paper.

In a small bowl, dissolve the instant coffee in the boiling water.

Place the butter and sugar in a large bowl and beat with electric beaters for 2–3 minutes until pale and creamy. Add the eggs, one at a time, beating well between additions.

Sift the flours, bicarbonate of soda, baking powder and xanthan gum (if using) three times into a bowl (or mix well with a whisk to ensure they are well combined). Fold the sifted flour, dissolved coffee and sour cream into the butter mixture with a large metal spoon. Pour the batter into the baking tin, smooth the surface and bake for 35 minutes.

To make the pecan topping, beat the butter, brown sugar, cinnamon and instant coffee with electric beaters until creamy. Stir in the chopped pecans.

After the cake has baked for 35–45 minutes, open the oven door and sprinkle the topping mixture evenly over the cake (take care not to burn yourself). Cover with foil and bake for a further 10–20 minutes, or until a skewer inserted into the centre comes out clean. Remove from the oven and cool in the tin for 10 minutes before turning out onto a wire rack to cool to room temperature. Dust with icing sugar before serving.

Upside-down Pineapple Polenta Cakes

Polenta is the key ingredient in these little cakes, giving a grainy texture that contrasts beautifully with the moist pineapple topping.

Combine the yoghurt, butter, sugar and vanilla in a bowl and beat with electric beaters until well combined. Add the eggs, one at a time, beating well between additions. Stir in the polenta, mixing well to ensure it is well combined. Cover and refrigerate for 3–4 hours or overnight.

Preheat the oven to 180°C and grease a 12-hole standard muffin tin.

Whisk the flour, coconut, baking powder, bicarbonate of soda and xanthan gum (if using) in a large bowl until thoroughly combined.

Add half the dry ingredients to the polenta mixture and beat with electric beaters on low speed until well combined. Add the remaining dry ingredients and mix well.

Place 1 tablespoon of pineapple in each muffin hole, then spoon in the batter until two-thirds full. Bake for 18–20 minutes or until firm to touch (a skewer inserted into the centre should come out clean). Cool in the tin for 5 minutes before turning out onto a wire rack to cool slightly. Serve pineapple-side up.

Makes 12

150 g low-fat gluten-free vanilla yoghurt
80 g butter, softened
1 cup caster sugar
2 teaspoons vanilla essence
3 eggs
1 cup polenta
65 g fine rice flour
2 tablespoons desiccated coconut
2 teaspoons gluten-free baking powder
1 teaspoon bicarbonate of soda
1 teaspoon xanthan gum (optional)
1 cup tinned crushed pineapple, drained

Decadent Orange Dessert Cake

This is a twist on the classic flourless orange cake. Ingredients such as red wine, star anise and cinnamon make this cake a delicious grown-up dessert.

Serves 10

¾ cup red wine

1½ tablespoons caster sugar

2 large oranges, cut into quarters, skin intact

2 star anise

1 cinnamon stick

6 eggs, lightly beaten

300 g ground almonds

250 g caster sugar, extra

1 teaspoon gluten-free baking powder

strips of orange rind, to serve (optional)

pure icing sugar, for dusting (optional)

Preheat the oven to 180°C and grease a 22 cm springform cake tin.

Combine the red wine, sugar, oranges, star anise, cinnamon stick and 1¼ cups water in a medium saucepan and heat over medium heat until the sugar has dissolved. Increase the heat and simmer, covered, for 30–40 minutes or until the oranges are soft. Set aside to cool. Remove the cinnamon and star anise from the syrup, and any pips from the oranges.

Place the orange quarters, syrup and eggs in a food processor and process until smooth.

Mix together the ground almonds, extra sugar and baking powder in a medium bowl. Add the orange mixture and beat well with a metal spoon.

Pour the batter into the tin and bake for 40–45 minutes, then cover with foil and bake for a further 15–20 minutes or until firm to touch (a skewer inserted into the centre should come out clean). Leave in the tin to cool completely, then turn out onto a wire rack. Decorate with orange rind and dust with icing sugar, or serve as a dessert with ice cream.

Panforte

This rich, dense treat is often reserved for Christmas, but I think it should be enjoyed any time, special occasion or not. It will keep in the refrigerator for up to a month. This recipe is not suitable if you are intolerant to sorbitol.

Makes 36 slices
¾ cup golden syrup
1½ cups brown sugar
2 tablespoons orange marmalade
100 g good-quality dark chocolate
1 cup blanched almonds, chopped
1½ cups pecans, chopped
¾ cup macadamia nuts, chopped
1 cup dried apricots, finely chopped
½ cup glace pineapple, chopped
½ cup mixed peel
2 tablespoons finely grated lemon zest
2 tablespoons finely grated orange zest
½ cup fine rice flour
½ cup cocoa powder
1 teaspoon ground cinnamon
1 teaspoon mixed spice
pure icing sugar, for dusting

Preheat the oven to 150°C. Lightly grease a 24 cm square baking tin and line with baking paper.

Combine the golden syrup, brown sugar and marmalade in a heavy-based saucepan over medium–high heat and stir constantly until the mixture comes to the boil. Reduce the heat and simmer for 5 minutes, stirring occasionally – the sugar syrup will become quite thick and foamy. Remove from the heat and leave to cool slightly. Stir in the chocolate.

Place the chopped nuts, fruit and lemon and orange zest in a large bowl and mix well. Sift the flour, cocoa powder and spices together and add to the fruit and nut mixture.

Pour the chocolate syrup over the fruit and nut mixture and stir until well combined.

Spoon the mixture into the tin and press flat with the back of a spoon. Bake for 25 minutes or until firm when pressed in the centre. Dust heavily with sifted icing sugar while hot, then cool to room temperatuare. Cut into slices to serve.

Glossary

BAKING POWDER

Baking powder is a raising agent. Not all baking powders are gluten-free – so always check the label before buying. A simple recipe for baking powder is 1 teaspoon cream of tartar and ½ teaspoon bicarbonate of soda. This can be added to 1 cup of a gluten-free flour blend to make it 'self-raising'.

BUCKWHEAT

Despite its name, buckwheat is not related to wheat at all – it is actually a member of the rhubarb family. It has a strong nutty flavour and is often made into flour and used in recipes such as pancakes.

CORNFLOUR

Gluten-free cornflour must be made from maize (corn). In some countries (including Australia and New Zealand) flour made from wheat can be called cornflour, so check the label. It has little taste, is low in protein, and makes an excellent addition to a gluten-free flour blend. It is perfect for thickening sauces.

POLENTA

Polenta (also called cornmeal) is ground corn. It varies in grades from fine to coarse, and can be used as an alternative to breadcrumbs, but is often cooked to a porridge-like consistency or firmer to make a cornbread. It is available in supermarkets.

POTATO FLOUR

Made from potato starch, potato flour is virtually tasteless. It can be used to thicken sauces in sweet and savoury dishes, however, the sauce will become a little 'stretchy' or gel-like. It is a great addition to a gluten-free flour blend, especially when being used for cakes and muffins, and makes a good substitute for tapioca flour and arrowroot. It is available in Asian grocery stores.

QUINOA

Pronounced 'keen-wah', quinoa can be used in a variety of ways: as pasta and flour; and as the whole grain, it can be cooked like rice and used as a basis for salads or savoury side dishes. It has a slightly bitter taste. Available from health-food shops.

RICE FLOUR

White rice flour is the main contributor to a gluten-free flour blend and is an essential addition to any gluten-free pantry. The texture ranges from gritty to fine – fine rice flour is preferable and is readily available in Asian grocery shops. It has a neutral taste and can be used as a thickener for sauces and gravy. Brown rice flour is also available and can be used in gluten-free baking to increase the fibre content.

SOY FLOUR

Soy flour is a high-protein flour made from soy beans. It can have a strong flavour, and is sometimes bitter. This bitterness decreases with cooking, but it is better to purchase debittered soy flour if possible. Soy flour is best used as a small but essential part of a gluten-free flour blend. It is available from health-food shops.

TAPIOCA FLOUR

Tapioca flour is made from the dried starch of cassava root. It has little flavour, is low in protein and is a useful addition to a gluten-free flour blend. It can be used to thicken sweet and savoury sauces, but the sauce will become a little 'stretchy' and gel-like. It is a good substitute for potato flour and arrowroot. Available in Asian grocery stores and some health-food shops.

XANTHAN GUM (FOOD ADDITIVE 415)

Xanthan gum is a vegetable gum used in baked goods to help provide elasticity and keep them moist. It is a cream-coloured powder made from the ground, dried cell coat of a laboratory-grown micro-organism called *Xanthomonas campestris*. It is the most common vegetable gum used in gluten-free cooking, though guar gum (food additive 412) or CMC (food additive 466) can be used instead. Available from health-food shops.

Acknowledgements

It is a hard task trying to thank all the wonderful people in my life who have supported me so enthusiastically, especially during the preparation of this book.

Without doubt, the members of my beloved family are the most special to me. I know how lucky I am to be surrounded by these amazing people, who believe in me and give me so much strength.

Special thanks to Mum, Linda, Jodie and Caitlyn – you four are absolute angels.

To Carolyn O'Gorman, a wonderful dietitian, friend and colleague who was tragically killed in the February 2009 Victorian bushfires. Carolyn introduced me to the gluten-free diet when I was first diagnosed 15 years ago, providing me and so many others with immense guidance and support. She was an inspirational pioneer who promoted all things gluten free. A beautiful woman who will be sadly missed.

To my very dear friends, old and new: Peter, Susannah, Steve W, Rohan, the Roses, Sharon, Claire, Dylan, Jason, Tim, Steve G, Dean, John, Amanda, Richard, Gill, Barb and the Pezzimenti clan. I love the good times we share – you are the best.

To my foodie friends who have helped and inspired me – heartfelt thanks to Tobie Puttock, Anthony Telford, Rosemary Stanton, Orio Randi, Spencer Clements, Jo Richardson and Homepride Fred.

Many thanks to the Coeliac Society, the Dietitian's Association of Australia and the Gastroenterological Society of Australia. Your professional support has been greatly appreciated. To my work colleagues – it is such a pleasure to share my days with you. Thanks also to my patients, who motivate me to achieve as much as I possibly can for people who have to live with food intolerances.

To the wonderful team at Penguin, I send you special thanks. You have acknowledged the needs of people with special dietary requirements, and enthusiastically supported me in my goal to promote the enjoyment of food. Thank you Julie Gibbs and Ingrid Ohlsson – it is a privilege to work with you again. I would especially like to thank Rachel Carter, my fun-loving editor, photographer Rob Palmer and stylist Jane Hann, home economist Jennifer Tolhurst, and Megan Baker for her brilliance in design (again!).

To the friends, colleagues and acquaintances who have not been specifically mentioned, I thank you for your very special role in helping make my life so fulfilling.

Index

A

Afghan biscuits 142
Almond and brazil nut slice 140
Asian duck risotto 53

B

Baked chai latte cheesecake 96
Baked custard with maple syrup 107
baking powder 154
Balsamic tomato and goat's cheese bites 6
bananas
    Banana hazelnut cake 132
    Caramel banana tart 102
Barbecued coriander and pepper lamb 74
Basic sponge 132
beef
    Beef and mushroom meatloaf 69
    Beef in red wine marinade 49
    Beef stroganoff 57
    Pasta bolognaise 72
    Shepherd's pie 57
berries
    Berries in liqueur syrup 96
    Cinnamon semifreddo with berries 90
    Lemon and blueberry friands 126
    Strawberry and cream cakes 121
    Strawberry coulis 101
biscuits
    Afghan biscuits 142
    Melting moments 130
    Muesli biscuits 139
blue cheese
    Blue cheese and walnut salad 40
    Potato and blue cheese soup 45
Brandy snaps with vanilla cream filling 104
Bread and butter pudding 117
Brown rice salad with goat's fetta 39
buckwheat 154
Butterfly cupcakes 144
Butterscotch steamed puddings 116

C

cakes
    Banana hazelnut cake 132
    Basic sponge 132
    Butterfly cupcakes 144
    Coffee and pecan cake 146
    Decadent orange dessert cake 150
    Fruit, nut and seed cake 135
    Moist family chocolate cake 122
    Strawberry and cream cakes 121
    Upside-down pineapple polenta cakes 149
Cappuccino creme brulee 112
Capsicum, haloumi and mushroom fritters 16
Caramel banana tart 102
Cashew, sweet potato and coriander dip 10
Chargrilled prawns with spicy sauce 14
cheese
    Balsamic tomato and goat's cheese bites 6
    Blue cheese and walnut salad 40
    Brown rice salad with goat's fetta 39
    Olive and fetta veal steaks 82
    Potato and blue cheese soup 45
    Rice-crusted cheese and bacon quiche 50
    Spinach and ricotta lasagne 82
cheesecakes
    Baked chai latte cheesecake 96
    Low-fat passionfruit cheesecake 95
chicken
    Chicken Parmigiana 70
    Chicken, mushroom and tarragon pasta 60
    Five-spice chicken stir-fry 77
    Satay chicken skewers 54
    Smoked chicken and wild rice salad 30
    Spicy chicken drumsticks 65
    Sweet and sour chicken 81
    Thai chicken salad 35
    Thick curried chicken and vegetable soup 44
chocolate
    Choc mint mousse 102
    Choc rough nut slice 136
    Chocolate rice pudding 108

Chocolate rocky road self-saucing pudding   116
Moist family chocolate cake   122
Rich mocha truffles   112
White chocolate panna cotta with hazelnut sauce   101
Christmas pudding   117
Cinnamon semifreddo with berries   90
coeliac disease   2
Coffee and pecan cake   146
cornflour   154
Creamy polenta   86
Cucumber, spinach and mint dip   8
Curried kangaroo   78

D

Date and ginger slice   140
Decadent orange dessert cake   150
dips
Moroccan carrot dip   10
Spinach, cucumber and mint dip   8
Sweet potato, cashew and coriander dip   10

F

fish
Salmon in white wine sauce   65
Sesame seafood stir-fry   69
Smoked salmon rice balls   20
Snapper, macadamia and lemon risotto   66
Five-spice chicken stir-fry   77
flour   154–55
food intolerances   2–3
Fried rice   87
fructans   3
fructose malabsorption   2
Fruit, nut and seed cake   135

G

Garlic and herb polenta bake   86
ginger
Ginger and date slice   140
Ginger pork noodles   58
Ginger syrup   90
gluten   2
goat's cheese
Balsamic tomato and goat's cheese bites   6
Brown rice salad with goat's fetta   39

Goodness salad   32
Grilled eggplant rolls   22

H

Haloumi, capsicum and mushroom fritters   16
hazelnuts
Hazelnut banana cake   132
Hazelnut sauce   101

I

ice cream
Lemon lime ice cream   98
Turkish delight ice cream   98
intolerances, food   2–3
irritable bowel syndrome   3

L

lactose   3
Laksa   45
lamb
Barbecued coriander and pepper lamb   74
Lamb and vegetable pasta soup   44
Spanish meatballs   62
lemons
Lemon and blueberry friands   126
Lemon custard tart   92
Lemon lime ice cream   98
Lime and coconut muffins   124
Low-fat passionfruit cheesecake   95

M

Macadamia, snapper and lemon risotto   66
Melting moments   130
Moist family chocolate cake   122
Moroccan carrot dip   10
Muesli biscuits   139
mushrooms
Beef and mushroom meatloaf   69
Chicken, mushroom and tarragon pasta   60
Haloumi, capsicum and mushroom fritters   16
Savoury mushroom bites   19

N

noodles
    Ginger pork noodles 58
    Noodle salad with Thai crab balls 29
nuts
    Almond and brazil nut slice 140
    Banana hazelnut cake 132
    Blue cheese and walnut salad 40
    Choc rough nut slice 136
    Coffee and pecan cake 146
    Fruit, nut and seed cake 135

O

Olive and fetta veal steaks 82
Orange and poppy-seed souffles 108

P

Pancakes with strawberry coulis 101
Panforte 152
pasta
    Chicken, mushroom and tarragon pasta 60
    Lamb and vegetable pasta soup 44
    Pasta bolognaise 72
    Spinach and ricotta lasagne 82
    Tomato, basil and bocconcini pasta bake 87
Pecan and coffee cake 146
Pizza bites 24
polenta 154
    Creamy polenta 86
    Garlic and herb polenta bake 86
    Upside-down pineapple polenta cakes 149
Potato and blue cheese soup 45
potato flour 154
prawns
    Chargrilled prawns with spicy sauce 14
    Vietnamese prawn salad 32
puddings
    Bread and butter pudding 117
    Chocolate rice pudding 108
    Chocolate rocky road self-saucing pudding 116
    Christmas pudding 117
    Steamed butterscotch puddings 116
    Vanilla sago puddings 104
pumpkin
    Pumpkin loaf 128
    Pumpkin pie 110

Q

quinoa 154

R

raffinose 3
rice
    Asian duck risotto 53
    Brown rice salad with goat's fetta 39
    Chocolate rice pudding 108
    Fried rice 87
    Rice-crusted cheese and bacon quiche 50
    Smoked chicken and wild rice salad 30
    Smoked salmon rice balls 20
    Snapper, macadamia and lemon risotto 66
rice flour 154
Rich mocha truffles 112
risotto
    Asian duck risotto 53
    Snapper, macadamia and lemon risotto 66
Rocky road chocolate self-saucing pudding 116

S

salads
    Blue cheese and walnut salad 40
    Brown rice salad with goat's fetta 39
    Goodness salad 32
    Noodle salad with Thai crab balls 29
    Smoked chicken and wild rice salad 30
    Spinach salad 40
    Tabbouleh 36
    Thai chicken salad 35
    Vietnamese prawn salad 32
Salmon in white wine sauce 65
Satay chicken skewers 54
sauces
    Hazelnut sauce 101
    Spicy sauce 14
Savoury mushroom bites 19
Seed, fruit and nut cake 135
Sesame seafood stir-fry 69
Shepherd's pie 57
slices
    Almond and brazil nut slice 140
    Choc rough nut slice 136
    Ginger and date slice 140
    Panforte 152

Smoked chicken and wild rice salad   30
Smoked salmon rice balls   20
Snapper, macadamia and lemon risotto   66
sorbitol   3
soups
   Laksa   45
   Lamb and vegetable pasta soup   44
   Potato and blue cheese soup   45
   Thick curried chicken and vegetable soup   44
soy flour   155
Spanish meatballs   62
Spicy chicken drumsticks   65
Spicy sauce   14
spinach
   Spinach and ricotta lasagne   82
   Spinach salad   40
   Spinach, cucumber and mint dip   8
Steamed butterscotch puddings   116
Stewed rhubarb in ginger syrup   90
stir-fries
   Five-spice chicken stir-fry   77
   Sesame seafood stir-fry   69
strawberries
   Strawberry and cream cakes   121
   Strawberry coulis   101
Sweet and sour chicken   81
Sweet potato, cashew and coriander dip   10
syrups
   Ginger syrup   90
   Liqueur syrup   96

T

Tabbouleh   36
tapioca flour   155
tarts
   Caramel banana tart   102
   Lemon custard tart   92
Thai chicken salad   35
Thai crab balls with noodle salad   29
Thick curried chicken and vegetable soup   44
tomatoes
   Balsamic tomato and goat's cheese bites   6
   Tomato, basil and bocconcini pasta bake   87
Turkish delight ice cream   98

U

Upside-down pineapple polenta cakes   149

V

Vanilla cream   104
Vanilla sago puddings   104
Vietnamese prawn salad   32
Vietnamese rice paper rolls   13

W

Walnut and blue cheese salad   40
White chocolate panna cotta with hazelnut sauce   101

X

xanthan gum   155

VIKING

Published by the Penguin Group
Penguin Group (Australia)
250 Camberwell Road, Camberwell, Victoria 3124, Australia
(a division of Pearson Australia Group Pty Ltd)
Penguin Group (USA) Inc.
375 Hudson Street, New York, New York 10014, USA
Penguin Group (Canada)
90 Eglinton Avenue East, Suite 700, Toronto, Canada ON M4P 2Y3
(a division of Pearson Penguin Canada Inc.)
Penguin Books Ltd
80 Strand, London WC2R 0RL England
Penguin Ireland
25 St Stephen's Green, Dublin 2, Ireland
(a division of Penguin Books Ltd)
Penguin Books India Pvt Ltd
11 Community Centre, Panchsheel Park, New Delhi – 110 017, India
Penguin Group (NZ)
67 Apollo Drive, Rosedale, North Shore 0632, New Zealand
(a division of Pearson New Zealand Ltd)
Penguin Books (South Africa) (Pty) Ltd
24 Sturdee Avenue, Rosebank, Johannesburg 2196, South Africa

Penguin Books Ltd, Registered Offices: 80 Strand, London, WC2R 0RL, England

First published by Penguin Group (Australia), 2009

10 9 8 7 6 5 4 3 2 1

Design by Megan Baker © Penguin Group (Australia)
Cover photograph by Rob Palmer
Styling by Jane Hann
Typeset in Delicato by Post Pre-press Group, Brisbane, Queensland
Colour reproduction by Splitting Image, Clayton, Victoria
Printed and bound in Singapore by Imago Productions

National Library of Australia
Cataloguing-in-Publication data:

Shepherd, Sue.
The gluten-free kitchen / Sue Shepherd.
978 0 670 07310 8 (pbk.)
Includes index.
Gluten-free diet--Recipes.

641.5631

penguin.com.au